THE
AFFIRMATIVE
ACTION
MYTH

THE AFFIRMATIVE ACTION MYTH

WHY BLACKS DON'T NEED RACIAL PREFERENCES TO SUCCEED

JASON L. RILEY

BASIC BOOKS

New York

Basic Books
Hachette Book Group
1290 Avenue of the Americas, New York, NY 10104
www.basicbooks.com

Printed in the United States of America

First Edition: May 2025

Published by Basic Books, an imprint of Hachette Book Group, Inc. The Basic Books name and logo is a trademark of the Hachette Book Group.

The Hachette Speakers Bureau provides a wide range of authors for speaking events. To find out more, go to hachettespeakersbureau.com or email HachetteSpeakers@hbgusa.com.

Basic books may be purchased in bulk for business, educational, or promotional use. For more information, please contact your local bookseller or the Hachette Book Group Special Markets Department at special.markets@hbgusa.com.

The publisher is not responsible for websites (or their content) that are not owned by the publisher.

Library of Congress Cataloging-in-Publication Data

Names: Riley, Jason L., 1971- author.
Title: The affirmative action myth : why blacks don't need racial
    preferences to succeed / Jason L. Riley.
Other titles: Why blacks don't need racial preferences to succeed
Description: First edition. | New York : Basic Books, 2025. | Includes
    bibliographical references and index.
Identifiers: LCCN 2024056283 | ISBN 9781541604551 (hardcover) | ISBN
    9781541604568 (ebook)
Subjects: LCSH: African Americans—Social conditions—20th century. |
    African Americans—Social conditions—21st century. | Affirmative action
    programs—United States—History—20th century. | Affirmative action
    programs—United States—History—21st century. | African
    Americans—Economic conditions—20th century. | African
    Americans—Economic conditions—21st century. | United States—Race
    relations—History—20th century. | United States—Race
    relations—History—21st century.
Classification: LCC E185.86 .R548 2025 | DDC
    305.896/0730904—dc23/eng/20250203
LC record available at https://lccn.loc.gov/2024056283

ISBNs: 9781541604551 (hardcover), 9781541604568 (ebook)

LSC-C

Printing 1, 2025

CONTENTS

Preface

The Supreme Court's 2023 ruling in *Students for Fair Admissions v. Harvard* declared it unconstitutional to consider race in college admissions. By that time, however, the practice already had been prohibited in nine states through lower-court decisions, actions taken by elected officials, or ballot initiatives put to voters. Moreover, those states with preexisting bans, including California, Florida, Texas, Michigan, and Arizona, were among the largest and most diverse states in the nation and thus offered some indication of where public sentiment stood prior to the *Harvard* decision.

Writing for the majority, Chief Justice John Roberts said that affirmative action policies in higher education, which have been promoted as a response to past or present discrimination, were themselves discriminatory because they used race and ethnicity to admit some applicants at the expense of others. "Eliminating racial discrimination means eliminating all of it," he wrote. "The student must be treated based on his or her experiences as an individual—not on the basis of race. Many universities have for too long done just the opposite." Fallout from the ruling was instructive. Among political conservatives the court had struck a blow for color blindness. The general public, which already had been tilting in that direction, mostly shrugged. But journalists, public intellectuals, and political leaders on the ideological left were beside themselves.

President Joe Biden said that the decision "threatens to move the country backwards."[1] Former president Barack Obama also weighed in, lamenting the end of a practice that he said had "allowed generations of students" like him "to prove we belonged."[2] And former first lady Michelle Obama, who like her husband earned a law degree from Harvard, expressed concern that race-blind admissions would result in fewer opportunities for minorities. "My heart breaks for any young person out there who's wondering what their future holds—and what kinds of chances will be open to them."[3]

Reaction to the decision in media and academic circles was likewise mostly negative. Joy Reid, an MSNBC host, said that racial preferences were the only reason black people like her had access to selective colleges. Eddie Glaude, a black professor of African American studies at Princeton, suspected that "we will begin to see a kind of segregated higher education landscape."[4] Another black academic, Jelani Cobb of Columbia University, wrote in the *New Yorker* that "the scale of what has been lost is difficult to assess," yet he felt confident in predicting that "the result will be fewer students from traditionally underrepresented minorities on college campuses, particularly at the most competitive institutions."[5]

If reaction among left-wing elites toggled between dismay and panic, the response from ordinary Americans—including blacks—was far more muted. According to the *Washington Post*, polls taken after the *Harvard* decision showed that the public approved of the outcome by more than two to one, "a finding in line with surveys conducted before the decision, including from the *Washington Post* and CBS News, which showed more than 6 in 10 Americans supported the idea of banning the use of race and ethnicity in admissions." Nor did the black intellectuals who objected to the court's ruling represent the dominant view among black people. An Economist/YouGov survey showed that 44 percent of blacks were in favor of the decision, while 36 percent of blacks were against it. And the share of blacks who "strongly" favored the ruling exceeded the share who strongly opposed it. Reporting on the results, the *Washington Post* noted that only 20 percent of blacks said that affirmative action had helped them personally. "And strikingly, significantly more—35 percent—actually said they felt such policies had put them at a *disadvantage*. This was more than any other racial group tested."[6]

Those findings shocked journalists who assumed that racial preferences are beneficial and more popular among the intended beneficiaries, but they didn't surprise scholars who had studied the history of race-conscious policies in the

United States. "Black Americans have had ambivalent feelings about affirmative action since its inception," according to Gerald Early, a professor of African American studies at Washington University in St. Louis. "Though the extent and implications of the policy have changed radically over time, it has never benefited more than a small minority of Black people."[7]

The myths surrounding affirmative action relate to both its popularity and its utility. And part of the confusion is the language used to describe group preferences, set-asides, and quotas. Determining whether someone supports affirmative action often comes down to the wording of the question. In a 1997 *New York Times*/CBS News poll that asked how equally qualified college applicants should be evaluated by admissions officials, 69 percent of white respondents and 63 percent of blacks said that race should not be a factor.[8] A 2001 survey conducted by the *Washington Post*, the Kaiser Family Foundation, and Harvard University was more detailed. "In order to give minorities more opportunity," the question began, "do you believe race or ethnicity should be a factor when deciding who is hired, promoted, or admitted to college, or that hiring, promotions, and college admissions should be based strictly on merit and qualifications other than race or ethnicity?" Ninety-two percent of all respondents and 86 percent of blacks said that those decisions "should be based strictly on merit and qualifications other than race/ethnicity."[9]

More recently, a Pew Research Center poll from 2019 found that 73 percent of all respondents, including 78 percent of whites, 65 percent of Hispanics, 62 percent of blacks, and 58 percent of Asians, said "colleges should not consider race in admissions."[10] And in 2020, a ballot initiative that would have reversed a 1996 referendum that prohibited state institutions in California from considering race in employment and college admissions was soundly defeated by voters.

Surveys that show majority support for affirmative action policies are far less common and tend to use more euphemistic wording. In a 2013 *New York Times* poll, for example, 53 percent of respondents backed "affirmative action programs for minorities in college admissions and hiring." But the story also noted that "other surveys that frame the question in terms of giving minorities 'preference' find less support."[11] In a 2020 essay, Frank Newport, former head of the Gallup polling company, elaborated on the "complexities of public opinion when considerations of affirmative action get down to specifics." He explained that when Gallup asked "a straightforward question about affirmative action without a definition or explanation—'Do you generally favor or oppose affirmative action programs for racial minorities?'" (as it did in 2018)—"61% of Americans were in favor, while 30% were opposed." The upshot is that large majorities tend to back the general concept of equal opportunity and improving the position of racial minorities in society, Newport noted, but "public support appears significantly lower when questions ask about policies that explicitly take race into account to achieve these objectives."[12] It seems that the more accurately you describe affirmative action as it has been utilized in hiring and college admissions in recent decades, the worse it polls. And that's true not only among the minority groups who have been the intended beneficiaries of these policies but also among the public at large.

If polling results on affirmative action can appear ambiguous, it may be because the meaning and use of the phrase has evolved significantly over the decades. Initially, the concept was applied to labor law, not race. The National Labor Relations Act of 1935, which guarantees the right of private sector employees to organize and engage in collective bargaining, said employers were obligated not merely to "cease and desist" from certain anti-union activities but also to take "affirmative action" to redress unfair labor practices. That could include, among other things, reinstating workers who had been fired for seeking to unionize, and posting notices that a company would not discriminate against union members.[13]

By 1960, "phrases like 'positive effort' and 'affirmative program' had become common currency in the lexicon of civil rights, especially among liberal Democrats," wrote the historian Hugh Davis Graham. John F. Kennedy's presidential campaign rhetoric "had been peppered with these kinds of allusions to more positive obligations. Their meaning was commonly understood to signify a more aggressive strategy for seeking out minority applicants, as opposed to the 'mere' passive nondiscrimination that liberal Democrats ascribed to the Eisenhower administration and to the Republican equal employment committees of the 1950s."[14]

The 1960s brought the passage of landmark legislation that guaranteed the equal treatment of individuals regardless of race. Yet during the same decade, the emphasis on outreach to historically marginalized groups shifted to an emphasis on racial balance in outcomes. Moreover, an absence of racial balance came to be interpreted as evidence of discrimination. "The expectation of color-blindness that was paramount in the mid-1960s has been replaced by policies setting a rigid frame of numerical requirements," Harvard sociologist Nathan Glazer later wrote. "Whatever the term meant in the 1960s, since the 1970s affirmative action means quotas and goals and timetables."[15]

The trend that Glazer described has not only continued but accelerated under various guises. Today, new forms of affirmative action include antiracism initiatives; diversity, equity, and inclusion directives; and slavery reparations advocacy (which will be discussed in a subsequent chapter). What all these concepts share is the use of squishy, inexact terminology—"antiracism," "diversity," "inclusion"—that can lend itself to multiple and sometimes contradictory meanings, along with an underlying assumption that the uneven representation of certain minority groups in a school or an occupation or an income bracket is self-evident proof of discrimination. The policy shift away from a focus on color blindness and toward treating race as a person's defining feature is being driven by politicians, activists, and intellectuals with self-serving agendas. It's a shift that has occurred despite the broad unpopularity of race preferences as evidenced by opinion surveys, and it is likely to continue for the foreseeable future, notwithstanding the Supreme Court's ban on affirmative action.

Before affirmative action can be discussed rationally, however, it helps to provide a working definition of the phrase so that people who disagree can do so without talking past one another. The focus in the chapters that follow is not on affirmative action in the sense of simple outreach to an underrepresented group, which is how the term was initially used. Some will pretend that this is all that the phrase continues to mean, but that's political spin and intellectually dishonest. After Barack Obama insisted, in his 2006 book, *The Audacity of Hope*, that "affirmative-action programs, when properly structured, can open up opportunities otherwise closed to qualified minorities without diminishing opportunities for white students," a Harvard law professor and prominent proponent of group preferences chided him for denying the obvious. "Acutely sensitive to charges that he supports racial favoritism that discriminates against whites, Obama defines affirmative action in a fashion meant to drain it of controversy," wrote Randall Kennedy. The reality, he added, is that "affirmative action *does* distinguish between people on a racial basis. It *does* discriminate. It *does* redistribute resources. It *does* favor preferred racial categories of candidates, promoting some racial minorities over whites with superior records. It *does* generate stigma and resentment. These issues cannot be hidden for long behind verbal tricks."[16] (Emphasis in the original.)

Kennedy's assessment is correct, and in that vein my focus will be on what affirmative action has come to mean in practice over the decades as administrative regulations and court rulings have perverted the doctrine's original intent. Today, affirmative action is properly understood as synonymous with racial favoritism, double standards, and preferential policies for certain groups. Unless otherwise stated, that is how this book will employ the phrase. Moreover, although affirmative action policies in the US have been expanded to apply to women and some non-black minority groups, the chapters that follow will primarily analyze how affirmative action has impacted the country's black population. And *minorities* generally will refer to members of groups that must be given preference in hiring or school admissions to reach their share of the larger population.

The main purpose of this book is to explain how affirmative action has failed. I tell the story of black upward mobility in the pre–affirmative action era, why it was happening, how it compares with black advancement since 1970, and why this history ought to inform our discussions of social and economic disparities in ways that it rarely does. Regardless of the various arguments and justifications put forward by supporters of racial preferences over the past half-century, the ultimate question is whether these policies have worked as intended and deserve to continue, or whether they have outlived any usefulness they once may have had.

Introduction

The 2016 historical drama *Hidden Figures* tells the interwoven stories of Dorothy Vaughan, Mary Jackson, and Katherine Johnson, three remarkable black mathematicians who helped NASA launch its space exploration program in the 1950s and '60s. Vaughan taught computer programming to scores of other women after World War II at NASA's Langley Research Center in Virginia and eventually became the agency's first black supervisor. Jackson initially worked under Vaughn and then went on to become NASA's first black female engineer. Johnson calculated the rocket trajectories for NASA's first human space flights in the early 1960s and helped land Neil Armstrong on the moon in 1969. Before John Glenn's historic Friendship 7 flight in 1962, he singled out Johnson to double-check the computer-generated trajectories manually because he was not comfortable depending on a machine's calculations. Once she had finished, he said he was good to go.[1]

The film's primary focus is the everyday lives of its heroines while in NASA's employ and how they coped with the ugly racist and sexist attitudes of the Jim Crow era. It was a hit with critics and moviegoers alike, many of whom were unaware that black minds had helped America win the space race against the Soviet Union. But *Hidden Figures* is more than a story about unsung math whizzes. It doubles as a story about black upward mobility in the postwar period—progress that was taking place notwithstanding all manner of laws, policies, and customs that openly discriminated against blacks. The movie is based on a book of the same title by Margot Lee Shetterly, whose father, a retired black NASA scientist, first joined the agency in 1964. Shetterly was raised in Hampton, Virginia, in the 1970s and came to know many of her father's colleagues. In her childhood world, scientists and engineers were commonplace. "That so many of them were African American, many of them my grandmother's age, struck me as simply a part of the natural order of things: growing up in Hampton, the face of science was brown like mine," she wrote.[2]

The book goes much deeper than the film does in assessing the working- and middle-class black communities that produced Shetterly's protagonists. Vaughan was born in Kansas City, Missouri, in 1910, had been taught by her stepmother to read before starting school, and graduated from high school as class valedictorian at age fifteen. She won a full-tuition scholarship to Wilberforce University in Ohio, the oldest private black college in the US, where she majored in math and graduated in 1929. A professor at Wilberforce recommended

Vaughan for graduate study in mathematics at the historically black Howard University, where the department was run by two black mathematicians who had earned their doctorates from Cornell University and the University of Pennsylvania. She opted instead to work as a teacher to help her family financially during the Great Depression. Vaughan taught for more than a decade before taking the job at Langley. "She once discovered an error in one of the math textbooks she used in her classroom and dashed off a letter to the publisher informing them of their mistake," wrote Shetterly. The error was corrected, and the publisher sent back a thank-you note.[3]

Mary Jackson was born in Hampton, Virginia, and earned degrees in math and physical science from nearby Hampton University, then known as Hampton Institute, in 1943. "Mary followed the family tradition of enrolling in Hampton Institute, which had graduated her father, Frank Winston, her mother, Ella Scott Winston, and several of her ten older siblings," wrote Shetterly. "The school's philosophy of Negro advancement through self-help and practical and industrial training—the 'Hampton Idea,' closely associated with Booker T. Washington, the college's most famous graduate—mirrored the aspirations and philosophy of the surrounding black community."[4]

Katherine Johnson, a West Virginia native born in 1918, likewise showed an early proclivity for math and was just fourteen when she completed high school and enrolled at the historically black West Virginia State College. "By her junior year, Katherine had tackled every math course in the school's

13

catalog and had been taken under the wing of a gifted young math professor named William Waldron Schieffelin Claytor, who created advanced math classes just for her," Shetterly wrote.[5] Claytor had earned his doctorate in math from the University of Pennsylvania in 1933. Johnson's other black mentor in college, the chemist and mathematician Angie Turner King, received advanced degrees from Cornell in 1931 and from the University of Pittsburgh in 1955.

Shetterly's thumbnail sketches of black America in the early and middle decades of the twentieth century may surprise readers in the twenty-first century who have come to associate black communities with crime, violence, underperforming schools, empty lots, solo parenting, and high levels of unemployment. The book is a reminder that black America once looked much different. When Vaughan first arrived in segregated Newport News, Virginia, in 1943, to start her job at Langley, she lived with Frederick and Annie Lucy, an older black couple in the city's East End neighborhood who owned a grocery store and took in boarders. "A larger version of what Dorothy had left behind [in rural West Virginia], the East End was populated by stable Negro families in well-maintained homes, thriving local businesses, and a growing middle class," wrote Shetterly. "On the corner of the Lucys' block, a pharmacist had purchased a lot with plans to open the city's first Negro pharmacy. There was even a brand-new hospital nearby: Whittaker Memorial opened earlier in 1943, organized by black doctors and constructed by black architects."[6]

This story of upward mobility among black people who were only a couple of generations removed from slavery and still living under legally enforced submission has received nowhere near the amount of attention that it deserves. "The idea that black women had been recruited to work as mathematicians at the NASA installation in the South during the days of segregation defies our expectations and challenges much of what we think we know about American history," Shetterly noted. "It's a great story, and that alone makes it worth telling."[7] She's right. It *is* a great story, and one with implications that go far beyond her immediate subject matter. It's a story that, wittingly or not, raises important questions about social and economic inequality today, what's driving it, and how best to address it. Vaughan, Jackson, and Johnson were by no means typical of that era, when college degrees were uncommon among Americans of any race and when most blacks were still poor and unskilled. In 1940, 87 percent of black families lived below the poverty line, and only about 5 percent of black adults were engaged in nonmanual, white-collar work.[8] These women were very much the exceptions to that norm, but they also represented a new black vanguard.

Between 1940 and 1960 the poverty rate for blacks fell nearly in half, from 87 percent to 47 percent. It is widely assumed that today's black middle class owes its existence and sustenance mainly to affirmative action and government welfare programs. But this gets the order wrong. The forty-point drop in black poverty occurred well before President Lyndon B. Johnson's "war on poverty" and other Great Society initiatives pertaining to education, housing, and health care that were launched in the late-1960s and expanded in the 1970s. It occurred before the landmark Civil Rights Act of 1964 and

Voting Rights Act of 1965 had passed. It occurred long before not only the election of a black president but before blacks had any significant political clout in Congress or had won mayoral elections in major American cities with large black populations. And it predated the affirmative action hiring and preferential college admission policies that were implemented in earnest in the 1970s. In other words, these black gains coincided with peak Jim Crow, when housing and employment were sharply limited for blacks, who were shut out of union jobs and many professions dominated by whites.

"The persistent exclusion of people of color from the white American mainstream after the abolition of slavery is an indelible blot upon this nation's history," wrote Harvard political scientist Robert Putnam and coauthor Shaylyn Romney Garrett in their 2020 study, *The Upswing*. Yet, "as we looked closely at a variety of measures spanning the twentieth century, two surprises emerged. First, progress toward equality for black Americans didn't begin in 1965. By many measures, blacks were moving toward parity with whites well before the victories of the Civil Rights revolution, despite the limitations imposed by Jim Crow. And second, *after* the Civil Rights movement, that long-standing trend toward racial equality slowed, stopped, and even reversed" (emphasis in the original).[9]

The pre-1960s trends among blacks are well-known to anyone familiar with the work of scholars such as Robert Woodson, Charles Murray, Thomas Sowell, Walter Williams, John McWhorter, and Shelby Steele. Stephan Thernstrom and Abigail Thernstrom's classic 1996 study of black progress, *America in Black and White*, predated Putnam and Garrett's by nearly a quarter-century. "In the three decades between 1940 and 1970, the proportion of black people holding white-collar jobs rose dramatically—from 5 to 22 percent of the men and from 6 to 36 percent of the women," wrote the Thernstroms. "By 1970 over a fifth of African-American men and over a third of black women were in middle-class occupations, *four times* as many as in 1940 in the case of men and *six times* as many in the case of women." Before World War II, black bookkeepers and stenographers and mail carriers were rare. By 1970 they were common. "In fact, the growth of the black middle class long predates the adoption of race-conscious social policies. In some ways, indeed, the black middle class was expanding more rapidly before 1970 than after," the Thernstroms noted (emphasis in the original).[10]

The point here is not to in any way downplay or romanticize the country's awful history of slavery and racial segregation, or to imply that racism is over and done with. Racism still exists, and I don't expect to live to see the day when it doesn't. The relevant question is to what extent does past or current racism, in whatever form it takes, explain ongoing racial disparities, and to what extent are racial differences in outcomes being driven primarily by other factors that don't get nearly the amount of attention that racial-bias explanations have received.

Discussion in the media and academia of how blacks living today are affected by the "legacy of slavery" and the "legacy of Jim Crow" is commonplace and unending. But there has been no similar focus on the legacy of Lyndon Johnson's welfare state expansions in the late 1960s, which occurred right around the time that many positive black trend lines began to falter. And there is almost no consideration of the track record of race-conscious policies that were justified by proponents as a way to expedite black movement into the middle class. Civil rights activists have little incentive to look beyond racism for an explanation of social inequality, because doing so would call into question the relevance today of organizations such as Black Lives Matter and the NAACP. Overemphasizing racial bias is in their self-interest. Similarly, prestigious colleges and universities are less concerned with producing black graduates than they are with protecting their brands. And those brands are enhanced by having more racial balance on campus, regardless of whether it serves the interests of black students who are admitted with lower standards and ill-prepared to handle the workload. Corporations likewise have a stake in race-conscious hiring and promotions insofar as hitting the "right" numbers can serve as a shield against litigation.

The data I highlight in the pages that follow are not difficult to track down or hard to understand, yet they receive relatively little attention in the mainstream media. Affirmative-action policies are considered well-meaning and tend to go unscrutinized by sympathetic journalists and others who believe that good intentions matter more than actual results. The exponential growth of diversity, equity, and inclusion (DEI) initiatives in corporate America and higher education following the death of George Floyd in 2020 is one of any number of examples of the disconnect between the intentions of race-conscious policies and the outcomes. Diversity initiatives, which elevate the salience of race in hiring, promotions, and college admissions to help underrepresented minorities advance, were fashionable long before 2020, notwithstanding their highly questionable effectiveness. One assessment of the literature, published in the *Harvard Business Review* in 2012, was titled, "Diversity Training Doesn't Work." According to the article, a study of "829 companies over 31 years showed that diversity training had 'no positive effects in the average workplace'" and that millions of dollars were spent annually "on the training resulting in, well, nothing. Attitudes—and the diversity of the organizations—remained the same."[11] In a scholarly paper published in 2018, sociologists Frank Dobbin and Alexandra Kalev wrote that "hundreds of studies dating back to the 1930s suggest that antibias training does not reduce bias, alter behavior or change the workplace." According to the authors, "two-thirds of human resources specialists report that diversity training does not have positive effects, and several field studies have found no effect of diversity training on women's or minorities' careers or on managerial diversity." Dobbin and Kalev were somewhat amused that colleges and universities persisted in offering mandatory training to faculty and students, "given that the research on the poor performance of training comes out of academia. Imagine university health centers continuing to prescribe vitamin C for the common cold."[12]

Advocates maintain that diversity training "can foster better intergroup relations, improve the retention of minority employees, close recruitment gaps and so on," wrote author Jesse Singal in a *New York Times* essay. "The only problem? There's little evidence that many of these initiatives work. And the specific type of diversity training that is currently in vogue—mandatory training that blames dominant groups for D.E.I. problems—may well have a net negative effect on the outcomes managers claim to care about."[13]

On college campuses, as even some adherents acknowledge, the DEI push has been not only ineffective but also counterproductive. Tabia Lee, a DEI administrator who in 2023 was fired from her position at De Anza College, a community college in California, after two years on the job, explained what DEI initiatives in the academy amounted to in practice. "On paper, I was a good fit for the job. I am a black woman with decades of experience teaching in public schools and leading workshops on diversity, equity, inclusion, and antiracism," she wrote. "My crime at De Anza was running afoul of the tenets of critical social justice, a worldview that understands knowledge as relative and tied to unequal identity-based power dynamics that must be exposed and dismantled. This, I came to recognize, was the unofficial but strictly enforced ideological orthodoxy of De Anza—as it is at many other educational institutions."[14] The problem was not that public opinion had turned against *diversity, equity,* and *inclusion,* as those terms have long been commonly understood. The problem, rather, was that DEI proponents were trying to change the meaning of these words in the service of advancing an agenda that most people otherwise oppose. Lee further explained:

As I attended more events and spoke with more people, I realized that the institutional redefinition of familiar terms wasn't limited to "white supremacy." Race, racism, equality, and equity, I discovered, meant different things to my coworkers and supervising dean than they did to me. One of my officemates displayed a graphic of apples dropping to the ground from a tree, with the explanation that "equity means everybody gets some of the apples"; my officemates and supervising dean praised him for this "accurate definition." When I pointed out that this definition seemed to focus solely on equality of outcomes, without any attention to equality of opportunity or power, it was made clear this perspective wasn't welcome. "Equity" and "equality," for my colleagues, were separate and even opposed concepts, and as one of them told me, the aspiration to equality was "a thing of the past."[15]

At its best, the civil rights movement was about demanding universal standards of treatment, regardless of race and ethnicity. The goal was to transcend race, not make it all-important, and blacks have made faster progress when color blindness has been the policy objective. By contrast, the focus of most liberal elites has been on demanding preferential policies for lagging groups, which has reinforced negative stereotypes, retarded progress, and produced a backlash. "Out of the maelstrom of the 1960s rose an army of race experts whose ministrations unintentionally helped prolong old racial tensions and foster new misunderstandings and anxieties," wrote historian Elisabeth Lasch-Quinn.[16] "The civil rights movement did bring a revolution to American life, but the forces of reaction—though often striking a liberal or radical pose—gave a new lease on life to the race-conscious behavior not entirely unlike the double racial standard that ruled under white supremacy." How so? "Racial identity theory, oppression pedagogy, interracial etiquette, ethnotherapy—these are only a few examples of the new ministrations of the self-appointed liberation experts," Lasch-Quinn explained. "That we have allowed the civil rights revolution to be hijacked by these social engineers is one of our best-kept secrets and one of our greatest tragedies."[17]

Ultimately, outcomes are what matter most. And this book argues that a half-century of racial preferences on balance—whether in the form of policies promoting multiculturalism, antiracism, or DEI—have been a hindrance rather than a boon for blacks, that equal treatment historically has been far more important than special treatment, and that affirmative action has been given undue credit for the black upward mobility that has occurred. The focus of liberal intellectuals in journalism and the academy on what whites have done to blacks in the past can leave the impression that black history in the US is little more than a chronicle of oppression. But black history is also about what a race of people managed to accomplish against all odds in the face of that oppression, and this history reveals inconvenient truths for those who claim that ending "systemic racism" is a prerequisite for black advancement.

ONE

Ain't Misbehavin'

The Politics of Responsibility

One of the more popular television shows in the mid-1970s was the sitcom *Good Times*. Initially, the series centered on a married black couple, James and Florida Evans, who lived in a high-rise housing project in Chicago with their three children. But the character who grabbed the attention of most viewers turned out to be the eldest son, seventeen-year-old J.J. As the seasons progressed, the writers of the show increasingly made J.J. the primary focus.

I was too young to remember the show when it originally aired in primetime from 1974 to 1979, but I do recall watching reruns as a middle-school student in the 1980s and laughing at the broad humor right along with the studio audience. I also recall that neither of my parents had any interest in the series. Mom and Dad were divorced and agreed about hardly anything, but they shared an unmistakable dislike of *Good Times* and made it clear to me that the reason was J.J.

Jimmie Walker, the actor who played J.J., had a background in stand-up comedy and portrayed the character as something of a buffoon. He channeled dated negative stereotypes about black people that were lost on me at age twelve or thirteen but were still fresh in the minds of blacks of my parents' generation. J.J. was bug-eyed, oversexed, and dim-witted. He was a preening, jive-talking goofball who flashed his teeth on cue and shouted "Dy-no-mite!" whenever he got excited about something. What later came to light is that the actors who portrayed J.J.'s parents, Esther Rolle and John Amos, also took issue with the character, and it wasn't because they were jealous that Walker had become the show's breakout star. Rather, like my parents, they viewed J.J. as an embarrassing and harmful throwback to the minstrelsy of an earlier era.

Good Times made entertainment history as an early example of a black two-parent family on network television, which was a major reason Rolle, a veteran actress, had signed on as the family matriarch. Initially, she rejected the role because her character, Florida, was depicted as a single mother raising a bunch of kids by herself. Before accepting the part, Rolle insisted that Florida be married to a loving husband

and good father, which led to Amos being cast as the family patriarch, James, who sometimes was unemployed and often worked two jobs to keep food on the table but who nevertheless was a devoted spouse and constant presence in the lives of his children. "I prided myself on producing the first black father on television," Rolle told an interviewer years later. "I wasn't going to be a part of continuing a myth that subjugated my people to nothing. I wouldn't help them perpetrate that lie. I knew I had a wonderful father; all the kids I played with when I was growing up had fathers. I refused to be the next black virgin with a pile of children and no man in sight."[1]

Amos likewise was sensitive to how the J.J. character would be interpreted by white viewers, which led to constant run-ins with the show's writers. "I felt like I knew more about what a black family should be and how a black father would act than our writers, none of whom were black," he said in a 2020 interview. Their perception of the black family, he added, "was totally different than mine, and mine was steeped in reality."[2] The creative differences between Amos and the writers were never resolved. Amos's contract was not renewed after the second season, and his character was killed off. After leaving *Good Times*, he predicted that the show "would revert to the matriarchal thing—the fatherless black family. TV is the most powerful medium we have, and there just are not enough black male images—which I think James Evans is—on TV."[3]

Amos turned out to be right. Rolle continued playing Florida after his departure, but she also continued complaining in the media about the writing in general, and the J.J. character in particular. "He's 18 and he doesn't work. He can't read and write. He doesn't think," Rolle told *Ebony* magazine. "Little by little…they have made him more stupid and enlarged the role," she added. "I resent the imagery that says to black kids that you can make it by standing on the corner saying 'Dyn-o-mite!'"[4] Rolle quit the show at the end of its fourth season.

The television industry is more concerned with ratings than accuracy, so it's easy to see where the show's creators may have been coming from. They had a hit series and a marketable star in Jimmie Walker. Whatever they were doing was working, whether or not it had the approval of other black cast members. "For a spell, J.J. became a pop hero and a favorite of kids around the country, who gleefully imitated him and bought J.J. T-shirts, belt buckles, and pajamas," wrote film historian David Bogle. "They loved the Dyn-o-mite line, which was heard in schoolyards around the country. For children, he was as unreal as Saturday morning cartoons; they loved the exaggerations, the wild getups, the stylized movements."[5]

Of course, it was precisely this image of blackness that drove Esther Rolle and John Amos to distraction. Based on their personal knowledge and experience, the J.J. character was not only insulting but off base, as was the notion that broken homes and female-headed households were the black norm historically. It's noteworthy that Rolle and Amos were born in 1920 and 1939, respectively. In each US census taken from 1890 to 1940, black marriage rates surpassed white marriage rates.[6] A 2012 Census Bureau report on marriage trends noted that until 1960, black men were more likely than white men to be married, and that the same was true of black women compared to white women until 1970.[7] As of 1960, two out of three black children still lived with two parents, and 71 percent of black women between ages fifteen and forty-four either were married and living with their spouse (51 percent) or divorced, separated, or widowed (20 percent). Just 28 percent of these black women had never been married, versus 24 percent of comparable white women.[8]

A study of black families living in New York City between 1905 and 1925 found that just 3 percent "were male-absent, headed by a woman not yet 30," and "five in six black children under the age of six lived with both parents."[9] The black economist Walter Williams spent part of his childhood in the 1940s living in the Richard Allen Homes, a Philadelphia housing project, where he and his sister were raised by their mother after their father had abandoned them. In a 2010 autobiography, he recalled that his family stood out because it was one of the few without a father present. "Back in the '40s the Homes were not what they would become—a location known for drugs, killings, and nighttime sounds of gunfire," Williams wrote. "One of the most noticeable differences back then compared to today was the makeup of the resident families. Most of the children we played with, unlike my sister and I, lived with both parents. More than likely, there were other single-parent households but I can recall none. Fathers worked and mothers often did as well."[10] As Williams noted, these trends would change dramatically in subsequent decades, a development that will be discussed in more detail in the chapters that follow. The state of black America in the 1970s—growing rates of crime, single-parenting, and joblessness—is often attributed to the aftereffects of slavery and segregation. But as we shall see, generations of black people living closer to slavery saw those trendlines moving in the opposite direction, and the "legacy of slavery" doesn't explain this retrogression. The relevant point here is that Esther Rolle and John Amos's recollections of a childhood full of stable black nuclear families and positive black male role models is supported by historical data, and their frustrations with *Good Times* were well-founded.

A related concern that was common among black people who came of age in the first half of the twentieth century was how they were viewed by wider society. There was a heightened alertness within black communities as to whether other blacks were behaving in a manner that was "a credit to the race," in the phrasing of the period. The black scholar W. E. B. Du Bois wrote that "the individual black workman is rated not by his own efficiency, but by the efficiency of a whole group of black fellow workmen."[11] As a long-stigmatized minority group subjected to stereotypes of moral, genetic, and intellectual inferiority, how blacks in general were perceived by others mattered immensely.

Black people, it's worth noting, were not the only racial or ethnic minority group in the United States preoccupied with their image. After Chinese immigrants began arriving in California in the mid-1800s to take part in the Gold Rush, they formed benevolent associations that addressed poor hygiene, prostitution, gambling, and other behaviors that helped fuel anti-Chinese sentiment. These associations, wrote historian Roger Daniels, "served to exercise some forms of what sociologists call 'social control': That is, they encouraged their members to conform to certain community norms." Similarly, Daniels added, Japanese associations in the US at the turn of the twentieth century "encouraged Japanese to acculturate: to adopt Western dress and, above all, to educate their children."[12]

The Irish immigrants who arrived in the nineteenth century had developed a reputation for drunkenness, violent crime, and other "dysfunctional habits of mind brought over from the old country," a political historian noted. When the Irish moved into a neighborhood, property values fell, and other groups often moved away. To address behaviors and attitudes that hamstrung efforts to assimilate, Irish charitable organizations, settlement houses, and temperance societies emerged "to improve individuals' conduct and to help people conform to the standards of the larger society."[13] Irish-American leaders of that period "tried to change the Irish way of life," according to another study of major ethnic groups in the US. "They were highly critical of their compatriots' alcoholism, violence, ignorance, intolerance, and general lack of adaptation to the needs of a modern economy and society. Many schools, hospitals, orphanages, and poorhouses were built by the largely Irish American Catholic church, which carried on social work among the poor and tried to protect the immigrants from unscrupulous elements."[14] Today, Americans of Irish descent boast above-average levels of income and above-average rates of homeownership, college-completion, and representation in skilled professions.[15]

Americans of Chinese and Japanese descent now out-perform whites both academically and economically. Nevertheless, efforts to adopt middle-class attitudes and behaviors didn't spare these and other minority groups from being targets of governmental or societal bigotry. At the urging of nativists, Congress passed laws that limited immigration from Asia and Europe. Chinese American children were forced to attend segregated schools. Japanese Americans were placed in internment camps during World War II. What assimilating to middle-class mores did do, however, was help facilitate upward mobility for these groups, despite the prejudices they faced.

Likewise among black leaders in the early decades of the twentieth century, the assumption was not that adopting productive cultural habits would magically end discrimination or make blacks immune to racist violence. Rather, they understood that hard work, thrift, and education were desirable ends in themselves, as well as stepping stones to the middle class notwithstanding the racial barriers in place at the time. Black activists advocated for equal rights without downplaying the accompanying need for blacks to develop the knowledge, skills, and other human capital that would enable them to realize their potential as productive citizens. "It is important and right that all privileges of the law be ours, but it is vastly more important that we be prepared for the exercises of these privileges," said the black educator and former slave Booker T. Washington. This was a pragmatic call for blacks to ready themselves for the future, regardless of contemporary racial attitudes. "No race that has anything to contribute to the markets of the world is long in any degree ostracized," said Washington.[16]

Well over a century ago, in his landmark 1899 study, *The Philadelphia Negro*, Du Bois already was observing that factors other than racial bias played a larger role in black-white economic disparities. If white racism disappeared overnight, it probably "would not make very much difference in the positions occupied by Negroes," he speculated. "Some few would be promoted, some few would get new places [but] the mass would remain as they are" until a younger generation began to "try harder" and shed "the omnipresent excuse for failure: prejudice."[17] These black leaders of an earlier era asked something of black people, and black effort wasn't conditioned on the elimination of white racism. As far as they were concerned, it was incumbent upon blacks to change their own lives for the better, and upward mobility was a function of adopting productive cultural habits as well as securing equal rights. The hurdles that black people faced during the Jim Crow era went beyond the racist laws in effect, and black leaders understood that ending segregation wouldn't necessarily address these other formidable challenges.

In important ways, the twentieth-century migration of blacks out of the rural South in search of economic opportunity resembled migration to the US from abroad. In both cases, groups from a peasant background (the Irish, Italians, and Chinese, for example) were challenged with transitioning to life in an urban environment. And in both cases, there was an understanding that assimilating to the behaviors of the preexisting population could help ease the transition. Large numbers of blacks first began migrating out of the rural South in search of higher-paying jobs and better schools during World War I. Between 1910 and 1920, Detroit's black population grew from 5,700 to 41,000. During the following decade, Philadelphia's black population increased from 134,000 to 220,000; Chicago's climbed from 109,000 to 234,000; and New York's went from 152,000 to 328,000.[18] A second and larger black migration from the South coincided with the start of World War II. Some 1.6 million blacks left the region in the 1940s and another 1.4 million left in the 1950s.[19] In both migration periods, one of the biggest obstacles for these overwhelmingly rural blacks was adapting to an urban environment. Another related challenge was shedding what Stanford University scholar Thomas Sowell has called their "redneck culture." American blacks had adopted deleterious attitudes and behaviors that have been traced to particular regions of England and Scotland, the ancestral home of many Southern whites. "In the antebellum South, as in the places where Southerners originated in Britain, such people lagged far behind people from other regions in education, business ownership, a work ethic, or professional occupations," according to Sowell.[20] In the prologue to Grady McWhiney's *Cracker Culture: Celtic Ways in the Old South*, Forrest McDonald wrote that "in each of the decennial censuses from 1790 to 1860, about half of the white population of the South was of Irish, Scottish, or Welsh extraction, and about half of the remainder had originated in the western and northern English uplands."[21] Sowell noted that these immigrants had been called rednecks in their home countries before ever arriving in America. They brought these cultural ways with them where they settled and passed them along to the surrounding population, which happened to include the roughly nine-in-ten black Americans who were living in the South at the start of the 1900s. Drawing from the writings of McWhiney, McDonald, historian David Hackett Fischer, and other scholars of nineteenth-century Southern culture, Sowell described the striking overlaps between white "redneck" culture and what would later become known as black ghetto culture. "The cultural values and social patterns prevalent among Southern whites included an aversion to work, proneness to violence, neglect of education, sexual promiscuity, improvidence, drunkenness, lack of entrepreneurship, reckless searches for excitement, lively music and dance, and a style of religious oratory marked by strident rhetoric, unbridled emotions, and flamboyant imagery," he wrote.[22] "While a third of the white population of the U.S. lived within the redneck culture, more than 90% of the black population did. Although that culture eroded away over generations, it did so at different rates in different places and among different people. It eroded away much faster in Britain than in the U.S. and somewhat faster among Southern whites than among Southern blacks, who had fewer opportunities for education or for the rewards that come from escape from that counter-productive culture."[23]

Long before the modern civil rights movement or the Great Society or racial preferences, black people took it upon themselves to improve their situation through education and hard work and by adopting the same middle-class standards of behavior that historically have helped advance other racial and ethnic minority groups. Black newspapers such as the *Chicago Defender*, and civil rights organizations such as the Urban League, "ran periodic lists of 'do's and don'ts' that were recirculated over time" and offered lifestyle advice to new arrivals from the South, wrote Isabel Wilkerson in her book about the black migrations, *The Warmth of Other Suns*. "Don't use vile language in public places." "Don't appear on the street with old dust caps, dirty aprons and ragged clothes." "Don't loaf. Get a job at once." "Do not keep your children out of school." "Don't allow children to beg in the streets." "Do not send for your family until you get a job."[24]

At the start of the Civil War, 237,000 blacks lived in the free states and territories, according to the 1860 census. Like Southern blacks, this far smaller black population in the North adopted the cultural sensibilities of the majority white population that surrounded them, with the understanding that adherence to certain mores helped to improve race relations and secure whatever social and economic gains they were making. Ethnographies of life in northern cities prior to the first migration are instructive. "The massive black ghettos that had become common in the major northern cities by the middle of the twentieth century were largely a post–World War I development," wrote Sowell.[25] According to a definitive study of Chicago's black population during the period, as of 1910 "there were no communities in which Negroes were over 61 per cent of the population" and "[m]ore than two-thirds of Negroes lived in areas less than 50 per cent Negro."[26] While "Negroes developed their own family and community life, there was considerable friendly social intercourse between colored and white people, and marriages across the color-line were not unknown," the authors added. "Within a generation after the Civil War the community of the free was accepted as a normal part of the city's life. The tradition became set that Negroes could compete for power and prestige in the economic and political spheres."[27]

Other northern cities where the black population would soon balloon due to an influx of rural Southerners saw similar developments. A study of New York City noted that at the turn of the century, "most Negroes live in what would be the present day midtown area" and that although "there were sections of Negro concentration within this area, no single large neighborhood was an all-Negro community."[28] By the late 1800s, Detroit had a significant black working- and middle-class population that included janitors, tailors, dockworkers, carpenters, and factory workers, but it also sported a growing population of black elites. "Most of the black upper class in nineteenth-century Detroit were in either professional, white-collar, or entrepreneurial occupations," wrote historian David Katzman in *Before the Ghetto*. Black "physicians, dentists, and attorneys had mostly white practices"—that is, most of their patients and clients were white—"and the managers and clerks worked for white businesses or were in government services." Moreover, the integration trends of this period for black elites included schooling. "The pattern that most separated the upper class was their social interaction with whites on a regular and equal basis," Katzman added. "Many of the elite had enjoyed a common educational experience with white political and economic leaders at the Detroit Hight School, the Detroit College of Law, the Detroit College of Medicine, or the University of Michigan in Ann Arbor."[29] Reporting on the state of integration outside of the South as late as the early 1940s, the black journalist Roi Ottley noted that even the "more than twenty-odd [low-income housing] projects in cities like Chicago, Pittsburgh, Philadelphia, Newark, Los Angeles, and New York are occupied by Negro and white tenants. Prophecies of race riots have failed to materialize. There is manifest pride in the upkeep and appearance of grounds and buildings, and there is an easy association between the races."[30]

Notwithstanding these advances, black life in the North was far from ideal. The same Jim Crow segregation measures following Reconstruction that were enacted by law in the South were often enforced by custom in the North. Black people living in New York or Philadelphia or Detroit enjoyed a better quality of life in the early decades of the twentieth century, but "better" is relative, and racial discrimination in those locales was hardly uncommon. "People in the North tend to look down on Southerners in the matter of discrimination against the Negro, and to pride themselves upon the civilized treatment accorded him in communities north of the Mason and Dixon's Line," wrote the black essayist George Schuyler in 1949. "The facts, unfortunately, give little cause for condescension or pride. The Negro is still pretty much a second-class citizen all over the country."[31] Schooling for the vast majority of blacks in the North provides one of any number of examples. Soon after the Civil War, "most northern states enacted legislation that prohibited racial segregation in public education," wrote Davison Douglas in *Jim Crow Moves North*. "Most northern courts, when called upon to enforce this newly enacted antisegregation legislation, did so, ordering the admission of black children to white schools." Yet "school segregation persisted in some northern communities in open defiance of law during the late nineteenth century. Moreover, with the migration of hundreds of thousands of southern blacks into northern communities during the first half of the twentieth century, northern school segregation dramatically increased."[32]

The upshot is that although Northern black communities were "acculturating to the norms of the Northern white society around them," wrote Sowell, "all of that changed radically within a relatively few years, as massive migrations from the South not only enlarged Northern black communities but transformed them culturally." He added that the "sheer numbers of these new black migrants from the South not only overwhelmed the relatively small black populations in Northern cities demographically in the early twentieth century, their very different behavior patterns shocked both blacks and whites at the same time."[33]

The Chicago Urban League "helped direct migrants to temporary shelter, rental options, and jobs," wrote Wilkerson. "It held what it called 'Strangers Meetings' to help acclimate the newcomers, and its members went door-to-door, passing out leaflets advising the migrants as to their behavior and comportment."[34] In a 1917 editorial, the *Chicago Defender* wrote, "It is our duty to guide the hand of a less experienced one, especially when one misstep weakens our chance for climbing." Black Northerners knew that their fate, whether they wished it or not, was linked to the fate of the black country folk headed their way, wrote Wilkerson, "and the city people feared that the migrants could jeopardize the status of them all." A poll taken during World War II found that a large majority of black migrants admired black Northerners and wanted to emulate them, while a majority of black Northerners "viewed the newcomers in a negative light and saw them as hindering opportunities for all of them."[35]

These tensions were neither unique nor surprising. European immigrants who had established themselves in America also expressed apprehension about new arrivals. When eastern European Jews began migrating to the US in large numbers in the late 1800s, they met resistance from German Jews who had come decades earlier and put down roots. These eastern European Jews, from whom most Jews in the US today are descended, dressed and worshipped differently, were far poorer and less educated than their German counterparts, and spoke Yiddish, a language that Jewish elites belittled. "In short, the eastern European Jews were an acute embarrassment to the German Jews in America," wrote Sowell. "Their numbers, ways, and concentration made them highly visible, alarming other Americans and threatening an anti-Semitic reaction that would harm the German Jews, who had quietly gained acceptance before." In the Jewish press, which was controlled by German Jews, the immigrants were described as "speaking a 'piggish jargon,' and 'slovenly in dress, loud in manners, and vulgar in discourse,'" Sowell noted. Nevertheless, "German-Jewish organizations made strenuous efforts to aid, and especially to Americanize, the eastern European Jewish immigrants. Schools, libraries, hospitals, and community centers were established to serve 'downtown' Jews, financed by 'uptown' Jews."[36]

A 1908 article by New York City police commissioner Theodore Bingham argued that crime was so prevalent in Jewish and Italian neighborhoods that the establishment of a specialized detective force was warranted. "Among the most expert of all the street thieves are the Hebrew boys under sixteen," Bingham wrote. "Forty percent of the boys at the House of Refuge and twenty-seven percent of those arraigned in the Children's Court [are] of that race." Historian Howard

Sachar noted that the Jewish press at the time was outraged by the article but "failed to rebut Bingham's figures convincingly."[37] The upshot was the establishment by Jewish leaders of the Bureau of Social Morals, which worked with law enforcement to address a Jewish-immigrant crime problem that was harming the reputation of all Jews. Over a five-year period beginning in 1912, "the police closed down no fewer than twenty-two poolrooms, sixteen drug dens, thirty-four shtuss parlors, thirty-three brothels, and scores of other criminal dives, and arrested and prosecuted their proprietors," wrote Sachar. "By the 1920s, 'Jews' and 'criminality' ceased to be interchangeable terms in the public vernacular."[38]

Similarly, Northern black communities that had experienced declining discrimination and some fruits of acculturation during the Reconstruction era after the Civil War worried about retrogressions in race relations if cities were overwhelmed with hordes of less-acculturated black Southerners. Blacks in the North responded by advocating what historian Evelyn Higginbotham has called the "politics of respectability." The concept "emphasized reform of individual behavior and attitudes both as a goal in itself and as a strategy for reform of the entire structural system of American race relations."[39] This was not an attempt to accommodate racism, Higginbotham stressed. Nor was it meant to minimize or replace the fight among blacks for equal rights. "Instead, the politics of respectability assumed a fluid and shifting position along a continuum of African American resistance," she wrote. Its advocates "emphasized manners and morals while simultaneously asserting traditional forms of protest, such as petitions, boycotts, and verbal appeals to justice."[40]

This two-pronged approach endured through the Jim Crow era and was central to the epic civil rights battles of the mid-twentieth century, when individuals such as Martin Luther King Jr. and organizations such as the NAACP paid at least as much attention to black behavior as they did to white behavior. "We know that there are many things wrong in the white world. But there are many things wrong in the black world, too," King once told a congregation. "We can't keep on blaming the white man. There are many things we must do for ourselves." He added: "I know none of you make enough money—but save some of it. And there are some things we've got to face. I know the [segregation] situation is responsible for a lot of it, but do you know that Negroes are 10 per cent of the population of St. Louis and are responsible for 58 per cent of its crimes? We've got to face that. And we have to do something about our moral standards."[41] These were not one-off comments from King, and they weren't unique among black elites of his day. He and other black leaders regularly championed personal responsibility and viewed it as integral not only to black advancement generally but also to the civil rights battles that they were fighting on the ground, day-to-day.

Consider the famous event that sparked the civil rights movement. Several black people living in Montgomery, Alabama, in 1955 already had been arrested for refusing to yield their seats to white bus passengers, so why did opponents of segregation decide to build a protest around the arrest of Rosa

Parks instead of the others? E. D. Nixon, the head of the local
NAACP chapter at the time, explained the reasoning this way:

> The case of Louise Smith. I found her daddy in
> front of the shack, barefoot, drunk. Always drunk.
> Couldn't use her. In that year's second case, the
> girl, very brilliant but she'd had an illegitimate
> baby. Couldn't use her. The last case before Rosa
> was the daughter of a preacher who headed a re-
> form school for years. My interview of her con-
> vinced me that she wouldn't stand up to pressure.
> She was even afraid of me. When Rosa Parks was
> arrested, I thought "this is it!" 'Cause she's morally
> clean, she's reliable, nobody had nothing on her,
> she had the courage of her convictions.[42]

Referring to Parks, King said that "nobody can doubt the
height of her character," and fellow activist Ralph Abernathy
called her "soft-spoken and courteous," someone who "had an
air of gentility about her that usually evoked respect among
whites as well as blacks."[43] Parks's character traits were considered just as important as her act of civil disobedience because perceptions mattered. This sensitivity to appearance and
comportment continued into the rowdier 1960s, when black
and white students participated in sit-ins and Freedom Rides
in the South to test compliance with Supreme Court decisions
that had declared segregated lunch counters, bathrooms, and
waiting areas to be unconstitutional. Demonstrators were

instructed to dress a certain way—women in dresses or skirts, men in sports coats—and were trained in how to respond without violence when physically attacked. "One of the most remarkable things about the Freedom Rides is that there were 436 riders and not a single incident of breaking the discipline," said civil rights historian Raymond Arsenault. "It's hard to think of anything more striking in American history than that." Under pressure from the growing protests and Attorney General Robert Kennedy, the Interstate Commerce Commission finally issued an order in 1961 that committed the federal government to enforcing a ban on segregation in bus terminals. According to Arsenault, "No other group had ever won such a clear victory for civil rights."[44]

Following the successful Montgomery bus boycott, which brought King national attention and marked the beginning of the modern-day civil rights movement, he continued pressing black communities to be mindful of their personal conduct even as they also fought for fair treatment under the law. "When the white man argues that segregation should continue because of the Negro's lagging standards, he fails to see that the standards lag because of segregation," King wrote in *Stride Toward Freedom*. "Yet Negroes must be honest enough to admit that our standards do often fall short. One of the sure signs of maturity is the ability to rise to the point of self-criticism." He added:

> Whenever we are objects of criticism from white
> men, even though the criticisms are maliciously

directed and mixed with half-truths, we must pick out the elements of truth and make them the basis of creative reconstruction. We must not let the fact that we are the victims of injustice lull us into abrogating responsibility for our own lives. Our crime rate is far too high. Our level of cleanliness is frequently far too low. Too often those of us who are in the middle class live above our means, spend money on nonessentials and frivolities, and fail to give to serious causes, organizations, and educational institutions that so desperately need funds. We are too often loud and boisterous, and spend far too much on drink. Even the most poverty-stricken among us can purchase a ten-cent bar of soap; even the most uneducated among us can have high morals. Through community agencies and religious institutions Negro leaders must develop a positive program through which Negro youth can become adjusted to urban living and improve their general level of behavior.[45]

One of King's closest advisors, a white lawyer named Stanley Levison, read a final draft of the manuscript and strongly urged him to omit such passages. "Levison's biggest complaint focused on the section of the book about 'Negro self-improvement,'" wrote King biographer Jonathan Eig. "Rather than urging Negroes to 'hold up the mirror' and consider how they might improve their own character, Levison said, King should focus on urging them to join the fight for equality."[46] But King understood, just as Booker T. Washington and W. E. B. Du Bois had before him, that it was essential for blacks to do both things simultaneously. "Indeed, if first-class citizenship is to become a reality for the Negro," King wrote, "he must assume the primary responsibility for making it so."[47]

Those attitudes would shift significantly in the post–civil rights era. Concerns with respectability politics, as a tactic, has fallen out of favor, notwithstanding its demonstrable effectiveness and popularity. Leading black thinkers today—in politics, academia, and the media—tend to give much less, if any, weight to the importance of black behavior in addressing racial disparities. Many argue that the primary responsibility for black outcomes lies not with blacks themselves but with whites, and that racism is mainly if not entirely to blame for black-white gaps in everything from income to incarceration to standardized test scores. Today, "respectability politics" is derided as ineffective and a waste of time. Studious black youngsters and other black people who adopt middle-class speech, dress, and behavior are accused of racial betrayal, or "acting white."

The scholar and activist Ibram X. Kendi rejects as racial bigotry the notion that there are any differences in conduct between black and white people. "Every time someone racializes behavior—describes something as 'Black behavior'—they are expressing a racist idea," he wrote. "To be an antiracist is to recognize there is no such thing as racial behavior. To be an antiracist is to recognize that there is no such thing as Black behavior, let alone irresponsible Black behavior."[48] The sociologist and commentator Michael Eric Dyson said focusing on black personal behavior and self-help is "classist" and "elitist." It can "only reinforce suspicion about black humanity" and it "lets society off the hook."[49] Dyson told the *New York Times* that the antisocial behavior of low-income blacks today, including the violent crime that typically targets fellow black people, was justified. "None of us want our children to be murderers or thieves," he said, but "most poor blacks don't have a choice about those things."[50]

Historian Leon Litwack wrote that nineteenth-century white racists "equated black success with 'uppityness,' 'impudence,' 'getting out of place,' and pretentions toward racial equality. 'He think he white' was the expression sometimes used to convey that suspicion, or 'He is too smart,' 'He wants to be white and act like white people,' and 'He think he somebody.'"[51] Today, however, the "acting white" criticism has come to be used by blacks against other blacks who are accused of racial treachery. The put-down typically is directed against black students who are conscientious of their studies, but "'acting white' isn't only about academics," wrote Stuart Buck in his history of the phenomenon. "As many commentators and scholars have pointed out, the 'acting white' charge often is targeted at how someone talks or dresses, rather than at academic achievement itself."[52] The anthropologist John

Ogbu, who published a study of blacks living in a middle-class suburb of Cleveland, Ohio, in the 1990s, wrote that black students "did not reject making good grades per se" but did criticize "other Blacks with White attitudes and behaviors conducive to making good grades."[53]

Buck dated this thinking among blacks to the post-1960s era and cited dozens of black scholars who said that the phenomenon was virtually unheard of in black communities prior to that period. Harvard's Henry Louis Gates lamented that black children today identified "making straight A's, speaking standard English and going to the Smithsonian" as white behavior. He added that "if anybody had said anything like that when we were growing up in the '50s, first, your mother would smack you upside the head and, second, they'd check you into a mental institution." Another black academic, John McWhorter of Columbia University, noted in 2002 that "black people didn't suffer from this until about 35 years ago. There was no such thing as the 'acting white' syndrome in 1910." Leonard Pitts, a black columnist and commentator, wrote of "marveling at how dramatically African-American mores have shifted" over the decades. "Where earlier generations thought of education as a weapon of advancement and shield of self-esteem, many in this generation think of it as cultural betrayal." According to psychologist Beverly Daniel Tatum, "an oppositional identity that disdains academic achievement has not always been a characteristic of black adolescent peer groups" and instead "seems to be a post-desegregation phenomenon."[54]

If black youth in more recent decades have adopted an "oppositional" mindset, it has been with the approval of many intellectual elites who excuse and justify behavior that previous generations once discouraged and condemned. In addition, the definition of "acting white" has broadened considerably. School administrators in New York City have been instructed that concepts such as "objectivity," "hard work," "individualism," and "worship of the written word" are hallmarks of "white supremacy culture."[55] A mathematics professor and former dean of the University of Michigan's school of education has claimed that math is a "harbor for whiteness."[56] In 2021, education officials in California discovered signs of "white supremacy culture in the mathematics classroom" of the state's K-12 public schools. These signs included what the officials determined was an unwarranted focus on "getting the right answer," teaching math in a "linear fashion," and requiring students to "show their work."[57]

Diversity consultants hired by school faculties, government agencies, university administrations, and Fortune 500 companies have distributed training booklets that list so-called white values, which include: "'The King's English' rules," "objective, rational, linear thinking," "quantitative emphasis," a "work before play" mentality, and "adherence to rigid time schedules."[58] In 2020, the Smithsonian's National Museum of African American History and Culture in Washington, DC, featured a "whiteness" section on its website. Belief that "hard work is the key to success," "respect for authority," "planning for the future," and "the nuclear family" were listed on a chart as vestiges of "white culture." The museum eventually removed the material and apologized after complaints from conservatives on social media. "Ben Shapiro described the chart as crazy and evil and said it 'suggests all pathways to success—hard work, stable family structure, individual decision-making—represent complicity in white supremacy,'" the *Washington Post* reported.[59]

Shapiro is a white conservative author and activist, but there was a time when that type of criticism would have reflected mainstream thinking among blacks. "The middle-class values by which we were raised—the work ethic, the importance of education, the value of property ownership, of respectability, of 'getting ahead,' of stable family life, of initiative, of self-reliance, et cetera—are, in themselves, raceless and even assimilationist," wrote the race scholar Shelby Steele. "They urge us toward participation in the American mainstream, toward integration, toward the entire constellation of qualities that are implied in the word individualism. These values are almost rules for how to prosper in a democratic, free enterprise society that admires and rewards individual effort. They tell us to work hard for ourselves and our families and to seek our opportunities whenever they appear, inside or outside the confines of whatever ethnic group we may belong to." Steele argued that this mindset among black leaders changed for the worse in the latter half of the twentieth century. "The particular pattern of racial identity that emerged in the sixties and that still prevails today urges middle-class blacks (and all blacks) in the opposite direction.

This pattern asks us to see ourselves as an embattled minority, and it urges an adversarial stance toward the mainstream and an emphasis on ethnic consciousness over individualism. It is organized around an implied separatism."[60]

Not even Barack Obama escaped the wrath of black commentators who wanted no public acknowledgment or discussion of rampant social pathology in black communities. In the 2004 Democratic National Convention address that brought him national attention, Obama said: "Go into any inner-city neighborhood, and folks will tell you that government alone can't teach kids to learn. They know that parents have to parent, that children can't achieve unless we raise their expectations and turn off the television sets and eradicate the slander that says a black youth with a book is acting white."[61] While campaigning for president in 2007, he highlighted the connection between poverty and single parenting. "We have too many children in poverty in this country and everybody should be ashamed, but don't tell me it doesn't have a little to do with the fact that we got too many daddies not acting like daddies," he said. "Don't think that fatherhood ends at conception. I know something about that because my father wasn't around when I was young, and I struggled."[62]

As president, Obama continued to sound these themes on occasion. "Keep setting an example for what it means to be a man," he told graduates of historically black Morehouse College in a 2013 commencement address. "Be the best husband to your wife, or your boyfriend, or your partner. Be the best father you can be to your children. Because nothing is more important." Obama praised his mother and his grandparents, who raised him, but said he never got over not having a father around in his youth. "I sure wish I had had a father who was not only present but involved," he said. "And so my whole life, I've tried to be for Michelle and my girls what my father was not for my mother and me. I want to break that cycle where a father is not at home—where a father is not helping to raise that son or daughter." Obama added:

> Just as Morehouse has taught you to expect more of yourselves, inspire those who look up to you to expect more of themselves. We know that too many young men in our community continue to make bad choices. And I have to say, growing up, I made quite a few myself. Sometimes I wrote off my own failings as just another example of the world trying to keep a black man down. I had a tendency sometimes to make excuses for me not doing the right thing. But one of the things that all of you have learned over the last four years is there's no longer any room for excuses.[63]

These and similar commonsensical remarks by Obama tended to go over well with most audiences, but he experienced heavy backlash from progressives in general and the black intelligentsia in particular. The veteran civil rights activist Jesse Jackson accused Obama of "talking down to black people."[64] Citing his speeches on black agency, Michael Eric

Dyson called Obama's presidency "a big disappointment to many of the black people who, like me, looked to him for leadership." The president, he said, "led from behind" on race matters and "offered lectures about failed black morality" to appease whites.[65] "As both candidate and president, Obama's speeches have tended to allay white guilt," wrote Johns Hopkins University historian N. D. B Connolly. "They have scolded African-American masses for cultural pathology and implied that blacks were to blame for lingering white antipathy."[66] Columbia University's Jelani Cobb agreed. "It has been Obama's consistent habit," he wrote, "to douse moments of black achievement with soggy moralizing, whether at the commemoration of the 1963 March on Washington or during a commencement speech at Morehouse College."[67]

In a 2013 *Atlantic* magazine essay responding to Obama's Morehouse remarks, best-selling author Ta-Nehisi Coates accused Obama of picking on black people. "Taking the full measure of the Obama presidency thus far, it is hard to avoid the conclusion that this White House has one way of addressing the social ills that afflict black people—and particularly black youth—and another way of addressing everyone else," he wrote. "I would have a hard time imagining the president telling the women of Barnard that 'there's no longer room for any excuses'—as though they were in the business of making them. Barack Obama is, indeed, the president of 'all America,' but he also is singularly the scold of 'black America.' "[68]

Obama was well aware of this reaction in certain intellectual quarters and thus may have dialed down such rhetoric as his presidency progressed. However, he did push back on occasion. "There have been times where some thoughtful and sometimes not so thoughtful African-American commentators have gotten on both Michelle and me, suggesting that we are not addressing enough sort of institutional barriers and racism, and we're engaging in sort of up-by-the-bootstraps, Booker T. Washington messages that let the larger society off the hook," he said in a 2014 interview. "I always tell people to go read some of Dr. King's writings about the African-American community. For that matter, read Malcolm X.... There's no contradiction to say that there are issues of personal responsibility that have to be addressed, while still acknowledging that some of the specific pathologies in the African-American community are a direct result of our history."[69]

Nevertheless, Obama was not above lobbing similar criticisms at black political opponents when it served his and his party's interests. In 2023, when Senator Tim Scott of South Carolina was campaigning for the Republican presidential nomination, Obama accused him of downplaying racism and using his personal biography to showcase America's possibilities for anyone who puts in the effort. In a podcast discussion with his former chief strategist, David Axelrod, Obama was asked about Scott's rhetoric on the campaign trail. "I listened to Tim Scott," said Axelrod. "Half of it sounds a lot like what you were talking about in the speech in 2004, and all of our speeches from that point on, which was: 'I'm living proof that we are making progress as a country. I wouldn't be here but for that progress.'"

Obama rejected the comparison and became defensive. He said that Scott's message was overly optimistic, and that his use of biography was inappropriate. Scott's campaign, said Obama, was better understood as part of "a long history of African American or other minority candidates within the Republican Party who will validate America and say, 'Everything's great, and we can all make it.'"[70] Barack Obama would have us believe that his own racial optimism was warranted, while Tim Scott's is evidence that black Republicans are sellouts.

Critiques of respectability politics—which might more fittingly be called *responsibility* politics—tend to come in two forms. First, the approach is rejected on grounds that it blames the victim for his or her situation and downplays the role of past and present racism in black outcomes. The implication is that people who care about black upward mobility ought to spend more time rooting out racial discrimination and less time worrying about how black people comport themselves. Put another way, these critics want the focus to be on white behavior, not black behavior. But as Du Bois noted well over a century ago, while eliminating racism is a desirable goal shared by all people of good will, it doesn't guarantee economic advancement if behavioral patterns play a bigger role in racial disparities than racism does. And if that was true at the end of the nineteenth century, it remains true today.

"If, by some miracle, we could get to zero racism, it is by no means certain how much effect that would have" on black outcomes, wrote Thomas Sowell in a 2023 study of social inequality. "People in low-income American hillbilly counties already face zero racism, because these people are virtually all white. Yet they have lower incomes than blacks."[71] Citing census data, Sowell elaborated:

> Even today, in the twenty-first century, there are counties in the Appalachian regions of Kentucky— Clay County and Owsley County—that are more than 90 percent white, where the median household income is not only less than half the median household income of white Americans in the country as a whole, but also thousands of dollars less than the median household income of black Americans in the country as a whole. A Census Bureau study found Owsley County to be the lowest-income county in any American state in 2014, and its population was 99 percent white.[72]

Nor is it true that the elimination of racial and ethnic biases has been a prerequisite for the social and economic rise of other minorities, as evidenced not only by the aforementioned experiences of the Irish, Jews, and Asians, but also by the experiences of black immigrants to the US from Africa and the West Indies.[73] If racial prejudice is the main cause of racial differences in outcomes, how is it that black people from Nigeria and the Caribbean have earnings that exceed the national average? Further, how could the 2020 census report that there are more than nine million black Americans with earnings above the white median?[74] Are racist individuals and institutions in the US giving these nine million black people a pass? The reality is that human beings have abused one another in every society down through recorded history. To condition black advancement on the vanquishment of racism and prejudice is to condition it on something humanity has never achieved, while ignoring example after example of minority groups who have surmounted these barriers.

A second, more fundamental criticism of respectability politics is that it simply doesn't work as a strategy for black social uplift because racial inequalities have persisted. "The politics of respectability has failed miserably," according to Ibram X. Kendi, "and so, hopefully at some point we'll... stop using it."[75] Jelani Cobb argued that respectability politics merely "confirms the long and ugly tradition that conflates blackness with laziness and poverty, and whiteness with virtue and wealth." Meanwhile, he noted, "the black unemployment rate has been reliably half... as much as the white one" and "black wages lag behind at nearly every level of educational achievement."[76]

An editorial in *Ebony* magazine took Cobb's argument even further. "Old school 'values' did not save us from the ravages of social injustice. A stiff upper lip and freshly polished shoes did not save our sons from extrajudicial murder," it noted. "Young women were beaten while wearing skirts three inches below their knees. It mattered not what we were wearing, but the skin we were in. So-called 'respectability' did not deliver a quality basic education in our schools nor did it puff up our tax bases. It did not undo…employment or housing discrimination."[77]

While it is undeniable that black-white gaps persist, it is also undeniable that black progress in America has been significant, both in absolute terms and relative to white progress, and it has been most significant for those who aspired to the middle-class attitudes and behaviors championed by proponents of respectability politics. Between 1940 and 1960, the black poverty rate fell by 40 percentage points as blacks left the rural South for better schools and higher-wage jobs in the urban North. Credit for this phenomenal poverty reduction cannot go to the Civil Rights Act of 1964 or the Voting Rights Act of 1965. Nor can credit be given to "war on poverty" social programs or affirmative action, since none of those things existed between 1940 and 1960. What did exist during that period were far higher black marriage rates—and far lower percentages of black children born to single mothers—than we would see in the post-1960s era, when respectability politics was falling out of favor with the black intelligentsia, and black activists were downplaying the importance of the traditional family.[78] Married people of any race or ethnicity are much less likely to be impoverished, and children raised in two-parent homes are much more likely to finish high school, attend college, enter a skilled profession, avoid contact with the criminal justice system, and marry before they have children of their own.

There remains a gap between black and white poverty rates, and some of that may well be the result of lingering racist attitudes toward blacks. But for more than a quarter-century, the poverty rate for black married couples has been in the single digits and lower than the national average. In some years, the poverty rate for black couples has been lower than the poverty rate for both blacks on average and whites on average.[79] Similarly, the labor force participation rate of black males is lower than that of white males, but among married black men it's higher than that of white men who never married.[80] And most people in prison were raised with either one parent or neither parent.[81] The question then becomes whether winding up impoverished or incarcerated is more a function of racism or more a function of family structure. Again, racists are unlikely to be giving a pass to blacks who are married or who are children of two-parent households, so racial disparities would seem to have more to do with behavioral patterns than with eliminating racism.

Professors Kendi and Cobb, and other skeptics, claim that the focus on cultivating a favorable image of blacks has become an impediment to progress, but white attitudes toward blacks changed dramatically for the better in the 1950s and 1960s, when respectability-politics stalwarts such as Martin Luther King Jr., Thurgood Marshall, and the NAACP leadership were at the peak of their influence. Surveying the polling data of that period, Stephan and Abigail Thernstrom wrote:

> In 1944 only 42 percent of whites believed that blacks should have an equal chance at getting a job; 52 percent said frankly that whites should "have

the first chance." By 1963 five out of six whites had come to accept the principle that employment opportunities should not be restricted by race. Similarly, support for school integration jumped from 35 to 64 percent between 1942 and 1963, for integrated public transportation from 44 to 79 percent, and for neighborhood integration from 35 to 64 percent. It has sometimes been suggested that federal civil rights legislation in the 1960s was responsible for the huge shift in white racial attitudes, but that puts the cart before the horse. Deep attitudinal changes created the political pressure responsible for the enactment of new law.[82]

As will be discussed in subsequent chapters, black-white gaps in homeownership, criminal behavior, and white-collar employment were likewise narrowing in the post–World War II decades, when black leaders were more attuned to how blacks presented themselves to the larger public. One lesson is that upward mobility of a racial or ethnic minority group is more likely to occur when it's accompanied by an attentiveness to self-regard and self-respect. Discouraging acculturation and assimilation in the name of racial solidarity is self-defeating. The social retrogression on display among blacks since the 1960s, from higher rates of joblessness and crime to fewer intact families, is not evidence that respectability politics doesn't work so much as evidence that it has been abandoned.

TWO

From Equal Treatment to Equal Results

How the Goalposts Moved

The *New York Times* published a story on public opinion of affirmative action in October 2022, shortly before the Supreme Court heard arguments in two cases that challenged the use of race as a factor in university admissions. After posing a series of questions to a dozen college students, the reporters were astonished by the responses. "For those Americans who assume that college students today are left-wing activists who aren't in touch with the real world, our latest focus group will be especially eye-opening," the article began. "Rarely have we been as surprised by a focus group as when we asked this racially and socioeconomically diverse group of 12 students whether they supported affirmative action in college admission. Just one person said yes."

Among the respondents was a white student who told the paper that affirmative action works to "otherize" the beneficiaries and negate the achievements of all minorities. She said students who didn't receive preferential treatment might say of those who did that, "'They're only here because of this.' And that could potentially be harmful." A black student added: "I think the biggest issue with affirmative action is that it implies that people of color wouldn't be able to get that position on their own." An Asian student remarked that racial preferences paper over rather than address the underlying causes of the academic achievement gap. "Affirmative action," she said, "really doesn't fix the overall socioeconomic disparities between the groups that lead to those problems in the first place." And another black student lamented that affirmative action policies allow minorities to be used as window dressing. "A lot of the time, what happens is on these campuses where people do push for diversity, and they push those few people in, now you have them plastered all over school posters and taking a fake-laughing cameo just so you could see 'Oh, look, there's a brown woman. There's an Asian woman here, the Hispanic woman there. OK, so it's diverse enough.'"[1]

That reporters at the *New York Times* were surprised by these reactions reflects the disconnect between the sensibilities of ordinary Americans and those of many in the mainstream media. The reality is that there was nothing especially surprising about what the students said. As previously noted, widespread skepticism of racial preferences is not new, including among minorities. In a 1977 Gallup poll conducted long before those students (and perhaps some of their parents) were even born, just 27 percent of non-whites favored "preferential treatment" over "ability as determined by test scores," while 64 percent favored the reverse. Whether the responses were broken down by race, gender, or income level, Gallup found that "not a single population group supports affirmative action."[2]

As the American population's views on race grew less bigoted and discriminatory over the course of the twentieth century, "affirmative action" grew less popular. By the mid-1970s, the concept already had come to be equated with racial favoritism and double standards, which is something very different from what it meant previously, when the phrase was associated with extending new opportunities to formerly excluded groups and bringing those groups up to existing standards. Polling shows that by the 1960s, there was widespread and growing support for more integration—in employment, education, and residential housing—along with skepticism toward racial preferences. Racial attitudes began trending in a more enlightened direction in the 1940s, according to historian Hugh Davis Graham. "It is clear that the civil rights movement coincided with a sea change in white attitudes since World War II, when national survey research centers began systematically collecting baseline data," he wrote. "From these longitudinal surveys emerged a consistent and indeed overwhelming picture of growing racial tolerance among white Americans."[3] Even in the South, where resistance to integration had been most pronounced, trends were moving in the same direction. In 1942, just 2 percent of white Southerners and 42 percent of white Northerners said black and white children should attend the same school. By 1972, the numbers had climbed to 70 percent and 90 percent, respectively.[4]

A 2016 analysis of racial attitudes noted that "since the mid-twentieth century when such questions were first included in national surveys, whites have shown dramatic increases in support for the principles of racial equality—things like support for equality in jobs, schools, and public accommodations."* But after "peaking in the 1960s and 1970s, support for things like government expenditures on programs to benefit blacks and preferential treatment in jobs have been at about the same—generally low—levels."[5] In fifteen Pew Research surveys taken between 1987 and 2012, only a quarter to a third of all respondents agreed with the statement, "We should make every possible effort to improve the position of blacks and other minorities, even if it means

---

* One potential problem that arises in these surveys is whether the answers reflect a genuine decline in racist attitudes or simply a decline in the acceptability of airing such attitudes. To address this concern, social scientists began looking at the use of offensive terms in private Internet searches. The findings generally square with the polling data. See, for example, Steven Pinker, *Enlightenment Now: The Case for Reason, Science, Humanism, and Progress* (Viking, 2018), 215–219.

giving them preferential treatment," while the proportion who disagreed with that statement ranged from 62 percent to 72 percent.[6] Understanding how affirmative action's meaning evolved over the past six decades goes a long way toward understanding recent racial tensions on college campuses and in the workplace. It also serves as a cautionary tale for what can happen when the judiciary and unelected government bureaucrats seek to undermine the desires and clear intentions of the voting public as expressed not only in surveys but also through their elected representatives.

The policies that later were transformed into racial preferences for groups got their start as efforts to secure equal opportunities for individuals regardless of race. The lawmakers who backed the landmark Civil Rights Act of 1964 insisted that the legislation categorically prohibit racial quotas and any requirement that schools and employers engage in race-balancing. The goal was not to replace a Jim Crow system that discriminated against blacks with one that targeted other groups. Rather, it was to dismantle de jure segregation and establish a doctrine of color blindness in accordance with the Fourteenth Amendment of the US Constitution, which mandates equal protection under the law.

The push for a national antidiscrimination policy that would culminate under President Lyndon Johnson began more than two decades earlier under President Franklin Roosevelt. The onset of World War II ended stratospheric unemployment rates stemming from the Great Depression, but blacks were the last to be hired by employers during the defense industry jobs boom of the 1940s. In response to pressure from labor leader A. Philip Randolph and other black activists who were threatening a protest march on the US Capitol if their concerns weren't addressed, Roosevelt decided to bypass Congress and act on his own. In 1941, he exercised his wartime emergency powers to issue an executive order that barred discrimination "in the employment of workers in defense industries or government because of race, creed, color, or national origin." He also created the Fair Employment Practices Committee, which included black and white members, to monitor hiring practices. The FEPC began its work by holding a series of hearings that were "designed to estimate the nature and extent of discrimination in American defense industries as well as to make employers and labor unions aware of the presidential order forbidding such discrimination," wrote historian Paul Moreno. The committee "revealed and eliminated many of the grossest manifestations of discrimination, such as racially marked applications, the assignment of minorities to menial jobs regardless of skill, discriminatory job advertisements, and recruitment from discriminatory schools or unions."[7]

Predictably, Roosevelt's executive order received blowback from lawmakers, employers, and unions who worried about federal intervention in matters normally left to state and local authorities, but it ultimately increased job opportunities for black workers. "The FEPC's powers were limited by lack of funding, bureaucratic infighting, and a cumbersome legal process," wrote historian Jennifer Delton. "Despite these shortcomings, however, its hearings and investigations began the important work of publicly identifying and discrediting discrimination." The FEPC's strategy, Delton added, was "to seek an end to racial discrimination in employment. The hope was that, in prohibiting discrimination, individual black workers would secure employment commensurate with their qualifications."[8]

Again, the FEPC and its civil rights allies initially advocated *equal* treatment for individuals rather than *special* treatment for certain groups, and they rejected the idea of establishing numerical racial quotas as counterproductive. "The NAACP was especially critical of any kind of quotas," Delton wrote. "Blacks were after all a small minority in most areas of the nation. If such quotas were adopted everywhere, it followed that blacks would be relieved of, or denied, positions in white majority areas, which were in fact most areas. Quotas created employment ceilings." In her history of black female mathematicians hired in the 1940s to work in a laboratory at NASA's precursor, the National Advisory Committee for Aeronautics, Margot Lee Shetterly wrote that it was Randolph's "long-term vision and the specter of a march that never happened that pried open the door" for black workers. And it was Roosevelt's executive action desegregating the defense industry that "primed the pump for a new source of labor" in the United States. Notably, no standards were lowered to hire these black women. Rather, they met the existing requirements for the job. "Nearly two years after Randolph's 1941 showdown, as the laboratory's personnel requests reached the civil service, applications of qualified Negro female candidates began filtering in," Shetterly wrote. "Nothing in the applications indicated anything less than fitness for the job. If anything, they came with more experience than the white women applicants, with many years of teaching experience on top of math or science degrees."[9]

Roosevelt's successors likewise took an active role in securing civil rights for blacks, with mixed success, even while Congress at the time steadfastly refused to enact laws that would mandate nondiscriminatory hiring practices. In 1948, President Harry S. Truman desegregated the armed forces, issued his own executive order on fair employment, and called on Congress to pass legislation "prohibiting discrimination in employment based on race, color, religion or national origin."[10] Next came President Dwight Eisenhower's Committee on Government Contracts, and then came President John Kennedy's Committee on Equal Employment Opportunity. Both of these committees were tasked with addressing persistent employment discrimination.

Meanwhile, the constitutionality of racial discrimination was being challenged in the courts, where there was movement, however fitful and guarded, away from the "separate but equal" standard established in *Plessy v. Ferguson* (1896) and toward a doctrine of color blindness that Justice John Marshall Harlan had articulated in his lonely dissent in the 8–1 decision. The Supreme Court's regrettable 6–3 ruling in *Korematsu v. United States* (1944) upheld the US government's internment of Japanese Americans after the attack on Pearl Harbor and represented a low point in the court's protection of civil liberties. Based on their race, people were detained without due process. The court deferred to the government's argument that national security concerns justified internment, but the majority opinion also noted that "distinctions between citizens solely because of their ancestry are by their very nature odious to a free people whose institutions are founded upon the doctrine of equality."* Four years later, in *Sipuel v. Board of Regents*, the court ruled in favor of Ada Lois Sipuel, a black applicant to the all-white law school at the University of Oklahoma. Thurgood Marshall of the NAACP Legal Defense Fund, who was one of Sipuel's lawyers, argued in his brief that "classification and distinctions based on race and color have no legal validity in our society" and "are contrary to our constitution and laws."

In subsequent desegregation cases, up to and including the historic *Brown v. Board of Education* ruling in 1954 that declared segregated schools to be a violation of the Fourteenth Amendment's requirement of equal protection of the laws, Marshall and his colleagues repeatedly invoked Harlan's dissent in *Plessy*. Harlan wrote that "in view of the Constitution, in the eye of the law, there is in this country no superior, dominant, ruling class of citizens. There is no caste here. Our Constitution is color-blind, and neither knows nor tolerates classes among citizens. In respect of civil rights, all citizens are equal before the law."

---

* Chief Justice John Roberts repudiated the *Korematsu* decision in his majority opinion in *Trump v. Hawaii* (2018). "*Korematsu* was gravely wrong the day it was decided, has been overruled in the court of history, and—to be clear—'has no place in law under the Constitution,'" he wrote, quoting Justice Robert Jackson's dissent in the case.

After joining the Supreme Court, Marshall (and the NAACP) later changed their position and advocated for race-conscious policies. The point to be stressed here is that most mainstream civil rights activists and their allies in the middle decades of the twentieth century embraced the principle of color-blind justice as central to the movement, and that principle is what attracted wider public support for their cause. The changes in law were preceded by changes in public attitudes. "The unavoidable fact is that over a period of some 125 years ending only in the late 1960s, the American civil rights movement first elaborated, then held as its unvarying political objective a rule of law requiring the color-blind treatment of individuals," wrote historian Andrew Kull. "Not only did nondiscrimination hold out the promise of black social and economic advancement, but the right of the individual to be treated without regard to race was strenuously defended as a moral and political end in itself."[11] Constance Baker Motley, an attorney who worked with Marshall at the NAACP during the 1940s and '50s, said that Justice Harlan's *Plessy* dissent was Marshall's "Bible," and that he "would read aloud passages" to his colleagues. She added: "I do not believe we ever filed a major brief in the pre-*Brown* days in which a portion of that opinion was not quoted. Marshall's favorite quotation was, 'Our Constitution is color-blind.' It became our basic creed."[12]

The Supreme Court's *Brown* decision had effectively overturned *Plessy*, but not on the straightforward basis that the

Constitution is color-blind, as Justice Harlan had argued in his *Plessy* dissent. Instead, the *Brown* ruling held that racially segregated educational facilities harmed the self-esteem of black students and thus were "inherently unequal," even if white and black schools had comparable physical facilities and financial support. Citing "modern authority"—a reference to social-science studies unavailable decades earlier when *Plessy* was decided—Chief Justice Earl Warren wrote for a unanimous court that separating black children "from others of similar age and qualifications solely because of their race generates a feeling of inferiority as to their status in the community that may affect their hearts and minds in a way unlikely ever to be undone." Therefore, the black plaintiffs' rights under the equal protection clause of the Fourteenth Amendment had been violated. The upshot was that schools had to be desegregated to meet the Constitution's guarantee of equal protection under the law.

Warren's rationale raised some eyebrows, even if most of the country—aside from whites in former Confederate states—agreed with the outcome. The court had ruled that segregated schools were "inherently unequal" and cited psychological studies claiming that segregated schools negatively affected the learning capabilities of black children. Yet in 1954, the year of the decision, an all-black high school within walking distance of the Supreme Court sent a higher percentage of students to college than any white public high school in Washington, DC. The same school, Dunbar High School, also had been known to outperform white high schools on standardized tests.[13] If the court was correct in its assessment of racially separate learning facilities, how could Dunbar High School exist? Nor were blacks the only ethnic group that had attended segregated schools. "The most casual knowledge of history shows that all-Jewish, all-Chinese, or all-German schools have not been inherently inferior," the scholar Thomas Sowell noted. "Chinese and Japanese school children were at one time segregated both *de facto* and *de jure* in California, yet they outperformed white children—and largely still do."[14]

The court didn't have to rely on social science studies. It could have ruled, as Justice Harlan's *Plessy* dissent had and as Thurgood Marshall and the NAACP were urging, that the Constitution is color-blind. It could have said that *Plessy* had been wrongly decided because racially segregated schools and other public facilities in the South were intended to keep blacks in a subordinate position and thus violated the Fourteenth Amendment. Warren pulled his punches and invoked "modern authority" for political reasons. He avoided making a direct attack on *Plessy* and the South because he wanted the ruling to be unanimous and he didn't want the court to get too far ahead of public opinion on racial matters, prompting a backlash. "Southern power in the mid-fifties did not stop at Congress; it sat on the Court," wrote legal scholar J. Harvie Wilkinson. "Justices as different as Hugo Black, the Alabaman, Tom Clark, the Texan, and Stanley Reed, the Kentuckian, would have resisted any opinion that pointed a finger back home." Warren was acting within certain political constraints, Wilkinson added. "Temperance and tact were the order of the day. Why inflame that region whose acceptance, above all, would have to be won?"[15] Decades later, reflecting on his reasoning in *Brown*, Warren said, "On the merits, the natural, the logical, and practically the only way the case could be decided was clear. The question was how the decision would be reached." The chief justice "did not accuse the South of having acted illegally or immorally in practicing segregation," wrote Richard Kluger his book about the case. "Had he argued otherwise, he would have distanced himself from Black, Reed, and Clark, at least."[16]

The court did not order that schools be desegregated immediately. Instead, it put off implementation of the ruling for more than a year and heard further arguments from state and local officials on how to proceed. Ultimately, it ordered the defendants to "make a prompt and reasonable start toward full compliance," and it authorized lower courts to oversee local desegregation plans and ensure that children were assigned to public schools "on a racially non-discriminatory basis with all deliberate speed." Despite Warren's best efforts, a backlash ensued. In 1956, more than one hundred lawmakers in Congress signed a "Southern Manifesto" that condemned *Brown* as "clear abuse of judicial power" and vowed to use "all lawful means to bring about a reversal of the decision." Resistance was such that in 1957, President Eisenhower was compelled to order troops from the 101st Airborne Division to Little Rock, Arkansas, to ensure the safety of nine black students attempting to integrate the local high school. And in 1963,

Governor George Wallace of Alabama stood in the doorway of the University of Alabama to block the entry of blacks. In 1964, a full decade after the *Brown* decision, fewer than 3 per- cent of black students in the South, where most blacks lived, attended schools with white classmates. In absolute numbers, more Southern black children attended segregated schools in 1964 than in 1954.[17]

Congress's response to Southern intransigence was to pass the Civil Rights Act of 1964, in the hope of not only acceler- ating desegregation but also spreading it to areas outside of education, such as employment practices and public accom- modations. In his exhaustive study of the period, historian Hugh Davis Graham recounted that black leaders in the early 1960s were growing impatient with the pace of desegrega- tion. Some activist organizations that previously had focused on pursuing equal opportunities for black people, including the Student Nonviolent Coordinating Committee (SNCC) and the Congress on Racial Equality (CORE), were becom- ing more radical in their endeavors. "Between 1961 and 1963 CORE's northern chapters...grew more militant, escalating their picketing and boycotts from retail chains to banks, the construction industry, and even to manufacturers," Gra- ham wrote. "Ultimately, they escalated their demands from nondiscrimination to preferential employment policies."[18] Boycotts in Philadelphia resulted in two dozen companies agreeing to implement racial quotas in hiring, "and the tactic quickly spread" to Massachusetts, Michigan, New Jersey, Cal- ifornia, and New York. In New York City, there were demands that "Negroes be given 25 percent of all jobs on city contract" and "25 percent of all state construction contracts."[19]

Just as the legal rationale for desegregation had shifted, the policy prescription was transforming as well. In October 1963, Whitney Young of the National Urban League, a leading civil rights group, published an opinion piece in the *New York Times Magazine* advocating a "temporary 'more-than-equal' program of aid for Negro citizens" to address "the effects of over 300 years of oppression." Young called for a "conscious preferment" of blacks in hiring and college admissions "to help them catch up" to whites. "To put it another way, the scales of equal opportunity are now heavily weighted against the Negro and cannot be corrected...simply by applying equal weights," Young wrote. "For more than 300 years the white American has received special consideration, or 'preferential treatment,' if you will, over the Negro. What we ask now is that for a brief period there be a massive effort to include the Negro in the mainstream of American life. Furthermore, we are not asking for equal time; a major effort, honestly applied, need last only some 10 years."[20] At a White House press conference earlier that year, President Kennedy was asked to respond to the growing nationwide debate over replacing Jim Crow policies with racial quotas. "[W]e ought not to begin the quota system," Kennedy argued. "We are too mixed, this society of ours, to begin to divide on the basis of race and color.... I think it's a mistake to begin to assign quotas on the basis of religion, or race, or color, or nationality. I think we'd get into a good deal of trouble."[21]

It was due to such concerns that when the Civil Rights Act of 1964 was being debated in Congress, supporters took pains to assure skeptics that the intent was not to replace discrimination against blacks with discrimination against whites. Rather, the goal was to ensure equal treatment, regardless of race, to people seeking education and employment opportunities. Title IV of the act concerns school desegregation and states plainly how the term "desegregation" should—and should not—be interpreted: "'Desegregation' means the assignment of students to public schools and within such schools without regard to their race, color, religion, or national origin, but 'desegregation' shall not mean the assignment of students to public schools in order to overcome racial imbalance."

Under Title VI of the act, institutions that receive federal funds—including colleges and universities—are prohibited from engaging in racial discrimination. Again, the wording is straightforward. "No person in the United States," it reads, "shall, on the ground of race, color, or national origin, be excluded from participation in, be denied the benefits of, or be subjected to discrimination under any program or activity receiving Federal financial assistance." Finally, Title VII of the act deals with hiring practices and prohibits employers from discriminating based on race:

It shall be an unlawful employment practice for an employer—

(1) to fail or refuse to hire or to discharge any individual, or otherwise to discriminate against

any individual with respect to his compensation, terms, conditions, or privileges of employment, because of such individual's race, color, religion, sex, or national origin; or

(2) to limit, segregate, or classify his employees or applicants for employment in any way which would deprive or tend to deprive any individual of employment opportunities or otherwise adversely affect his status as an employee, because of such individual's race, color, religion, sex, or national origin.

During the floor debates, Representative Emanuel Celler of New York, a leading proponent of the act, assured his colleagues that it contained "no authorization" for mandating "racial balance in given schools." Over in the Senate, Robert Byrd of West Virginia, who was against the act, wanted assurance that "school children may not be bused from one end of the community to another end of the community at taxpayers' expense to relieve so-called racial imbalance in the schools."[22] Hubert Humphrey of Minnesota, who guided the legislation through the Senate, attempted to allay Byrd's concerns. "[W]hile the Constitution prohibits segregation, it does not require integration," Humphrey said. "The busing of children to achieve racial balance would be an act to effect the integration of schools. In fact, if the bill were to compel it, it would be a violation, because it would be handling the matter on the basis of race and we would be transporting children because of race. The bill does not attempt to integrate the schools, but it does attempt to eliminate segregation in the school systems."[23]

Byrd remained skeptical and speculated that a court might order schools to integrate or that the federal Office of Education—a predecessor to the Department of Education—might threaten to cut funding for schools that weren't racially mixed. "Suppose the Office of Education establishes a regulation that there shall be no racial imbalance in the schools of any district which receives Federal assistance," he said.[24] Humphrey replied that nothing in the legislation empowered federal officials or courts to do that. Senator Jacob Javits of New York, who had helped draft the act, told Byrd that there was no "danger of envisaging the rule or regulation relating to racial imbalance" because "it is negated expressly in the bill." He added that any government official who tried to cite the act in support of racial balancing would be "making a fool of himself."

With respect to Title VII's employment provisions, opponents were concerned that the bill would force businesses to hire and promote less qualified blacks over more qualified whites. "We may be sure that whether it is imposed in the open regulation or not, in the actual administration of the proposal…the end result will be job preference in every instance for those belonging to the minority groups," said Senator Richard Russell Jr. of Georgia.[25] Again and again, supporters of the bill pushed back. To address the concerns of detractors, the legislation created a new federal agency, the Equal Employment Opportunity Commission (EEOC), that would oversee Title VII's employment provisions. Humphrey told his fellow senators that the act "does not provide that any preferential treatment in employment shall be given to Negroes or to any other persons or groups. It does not provide that any quota system may be established to maintain racial balance in employment. In fact, the title would prohibit preferential treatment for any particular group, and any person."[26] In a joint statement, Senators Joseph Clark of Pennsylvania and Clifford Case of New Jersey were no less emphatic:

> There is no requirement in Title VII that an employer maintain a racial balance in his work force. On the contrary, any deliberate attempt to maintain a racial balance, whatever such a balance may be, would involve a violation of Title VII because maintaining such a balance would require an employer to hire or refuse to hire on the basis of race. It must be emphasized that discrimination is prohibited as to any individual.[27]

Of course, Senators Robert Byrd and Richard Russell Jr. were committed segregationists who were never going to support the bill, even though language was inserted to address their concerns. They would go on to lead Southern opposition to the Civil Rights Act of 1964 as well as the Voting Rights Act of 1965.* Nevertheless, wrote journalist

---

* Later in life, Byrd, who died in 2010, expressed remorse for his earlier support of racial segregation.

Christopher Caldwell, the lawmakers "who opposed the legislation proved wiser about its consequences than those who sponsored it."[28] Within a decade the courts had approved compulsory busing to achieve racial balance in schools, and the EEOC had rewritten the legal standard for determining employment discrimination.

The back and forth between advocates and opponents is worth rehashing because it is a window into what Congress had intended. Thanks to this paper trail, we know that when the act referred to desegregation it meant assigning students to schools in a race-blind manner, not forced integration or numerical racial balancing. And when the act discussed discrimination, it meant intentional discrimination, and that discriminatory intent could *not* be inferred from racially disparate *outcomes* in the hiring and promotion of minorities. It's also clear that many of the later controversies over affirmative action stem directly from *redefining* these terms and ignoring the expressed wishes of the act's advocates. "In the whole of the congressional debate over the Civil Rights Act of 1964, no theme is more prominent than the exasperated insistence of the bill's supporters, in answer to repeated southern fears, that a law prohibiting discrimination must necessarily prohibit preferential treatment," wrote historian Andrew Kull. "Had the Senate been left in any doubt on this point, the Civil Rights Act of 1964 would not have been passed."[29]

Despite the strenuous efforts of opponents, which included a fourteen-hour filibuster by Senator Byrd, the colorblind consensus won the day. The Civil Rights Act passed both chambers of Congress by comfortable margins and was signed into law by President Lyndon Johnson on July 2, 1964. The vote in the House was 290–130, and the Senate tally was 73–27. Notably, a higher percentage of Republicans than Democrats in both chambers supported the act. As *Time* magazine reported, "In one of the most lopsidedly Democratic Houses since the days of F.D.R., Republicans were vital to the passage of a bill for which the Democratic administration means to take full political credit this year."[30] Ten years after the momentous ruling in *Brown*, the legislative and executive branches had struck a bipartisan blow against Jim Crow and had done so with the support of most of the country. By 1963, a majority of the public—54 percent versus 38 percent—were convinced that "racial practices were so intolerable that federal intervention was required," wrote the scholars Stephan Thernstrom and Abigail Thernstrom. "By February 1964, proponents of federal antidiscrimination legislation outnumbered opponents by two to one (61 versus 31 percent). Among northern whites, the ratio was more than three to one (71 versus 21 percent)."[31]

The passage of the Civil Rights Act of 1964 reflected public opinion, in other words, which showed large and growing support for race-blind policies both in education and employment. But there was no similar public consensus for what came next, which was an effort by willful federal bureaucrats and activist judges to ignore the actual language of the law, redefine terms such as *discrimination* and *desegregation* to their own liking, and advance an agenda of compulsory

integration and racial preferences in hiring. "Despite the legislative history and the repeated provisions of the 1964 Civil
Rights Act that racial discrimination was prohibited and
that no requirement of integration or racial balance was to
be imposed pursuant to the act, just such a requirement was
soon imposed by the Office of Education and upheld by the
courts," wrote legal scholar Lino Graglia. "A clearer illustration of administrative and judicial perversion of legislative
purpose would be difficult to find."[32] Graglia linked the subsequent judicial activism to *Brown*, a correct decision based
on sloppy arguments made out of political expediency. "As
important as that case is for its holding, it is far more important because it basically changed the views of the country, and
specifically of judges, as to the proper role of judges in our
system of government," he wrote. "*Brown* was less a traditional lawsuit than an attempt to bring about a social revolution through the Courts. The success of the revolution, some
ten years later (with the adoption of the 1964 Civil Rights
Act, endorsing and making effective *Brown*'s prohibition of
racial discrimination), inevitably led to the belief that there is
nothing that courts cannot or should not do."[33]

Under the Civil Rights Act of 1964, federal officials were
prohibited from issuing rules and regulations without the
president's approval. To skirt that requirement, the Office of
Education began issuing "administrative guidelines" for determining whether a school district was in compliance with
the law. In practice, these "guidelines" were rules and regulations in everything but name. The act defined *desegregation*

as no longer assigning students to schools based on skin color, and it prohibited racial balancing. But through the issuing of "guidelines," federal administrators were able to ignore the requirement in *Brown* and the Civil Rights Act of 1964 that officials not place children in school by race. Moreover, the judiciary went along with the scheme. "The Court of Appeals for the Fifth Circuit, by far the most important court of appeals for the school segregation litigation because of its jurisdiction over most of the deep South, quickly accepted the guidelines as establishing not only administrative requirements but also minimum constitutional requirements," Graglia wrote. "Consequently, the decisions of the judicial and administrative institutions thereafter had a cumulative and accelerating effect on the development of school segregation law."[34]

By 1966, just two years after the act's passage, terms such as *segregation* and *desegregation* had been given new meanings. One Office of Education guideline stated: "A school system may (1) permit any student to transfer from a school where students of his race are a majority to any other school, within the system, where students of his race are in the minority, or (2) assign students on such a basis."[35] The lawmakers who supported the 1964 Civil Rights Act were counting on the courts to serve as a check on such blatant distortions of the legislation, but that is not what happened. Instead, the Fifth Circuit blessed the new guidelines when it ruled in *United States v. Jefferson County Board of Education* (1966). "In this opinion," wrote Judge John Wisdom, "we use the words 'integration' and

THE AFFIRMATIVE ACTION MYTH

'desegregation' interchangeably." He dismissed distinctions between the two as "a quibble devised over ten years ago" by a misreading of *Brown* and added: "As we see it, the law imposes an absolute duty to desegregate, that is, disestablish segregation. And an absolute duty to integrate, in the sense that a disproportionate concentration of Negroes in certain schools cannot be ignored; racial mixing of students is a high priority educational goal."

Brown simply prohibited compulsory racial separation. It didn't mandate integration. What determined whether a "white school" was "desegregated" was whether black students were now permitted to enroll there, not whether blacks exercised that right. "By means of nothing more than wordplay," wrote Graglia, the Fifth Circuit held that "a requirement of integration was authorized by the 1964 act." By declining to review the *Jefferson* decision and permitting it to stand, the Supreme Court had sanctioned a new legal definition of *desegregation*. "Instead of providing a restraint on the excesses of other government officials—a traditional justification for the Supreme Court's extraordinary power in our system—the Court proved itself to be the most dangerous source of excess."[36] The Supreme Court's unanimous decision in *Green v. School Board of New Kent County* (1968), made the reinterpretation of *Brown* official. The case concerned a school desegregation plan in rural Virginia. Kent County had just two schools, one traditionally black and the other traditionally white. Although the district had formally declared that students of any race were free to attend either school, the black school had remained 85 percent black. On that basis, the court struck down the county's desegregation plan. Local authorities, it ruled, now had "an affirmative duty" to eliminate "dual" school systems. Moreover, for the first time the court cited a statistic—the fact that only 15 percent of blacks attended the white school—to justify its decision. "In other words, statistical *results* defined segregation," wrote the scholar Thomas Sowell. "*Green* was in many ways as decisive a case as *Brown*," he added. "It opened the era of court-ordered busing to remedy racial imbalance. The Court and its supporters represented this as simply speeding up the process begun long before under the doctrine of 'all deliberate speed'.... In reality, however, it was a substitution for a very different process—one in which children were to be assigned to schools by race instead of *without regard to race*."[37]

J. Harvie Wilkinson wrote that the *Green* ruling's "open use of a statistic" to reject a desegregation plan "had limitless implications" in other contexts:

> How far beyond ... public schools would the Court carry statistical reliance? Might an employer be in violation of the 1964 Civil Rights Act if his work force was 75 percent white? Or a criminal conviction be reversed if the jury was but 8 percent black? Or a zoning ordinance overturned if residents of the community were 95 percent white? Or legislative redistricting invalidated if few blacks were elected? Possibilities were endless. *Green* hardly

foreshadowed an enslavement to statistics...but numbers were definitely encouraged as future evidence of racial discrimination.[38]

It turned out that the judiciary and administrative state were willing to go quite far in sanctioning the use of statistical disparities as evidence of racial discrimination as well as the use of race-conscious remedies to address racial imbalances in schools and the workplace. In 1965, President Johnson issued an executive order that created the Office of Federal Contract Compliance and directed federal contractors to "take affirmative action" to ensure equal opportunity in their hiring practices. "At the time, that meant aggressive recruitment—making extra efforts to locate black talent that had been overlooked and to give that talent the chance to develop," wrote Stephan and Abigail Thernstrom. "But within four years, more color-conscious programs were in place. The administration's Equal Employment Opportunity Commission likewise rewrote the legal standards by which employment discrimination was to be judged, and laid the groundwork for 'disparate impact' cases that invited racial quotas in hiring."[39] Steadily, the burden on employers shifted from ensuring opportunity to all groups to ensuring representation of certain groups. Guidelines for government contractors issued in 1970 noted that an "affirmative action program is a set of specific and result-oriented procedures to which a contractor commits himself." And in 1971, for the first time, the federal guidelines stipulated that an "acceptable affirmative action program must include" not simply equal employment opportunities and hiring without regard to race, but also actual "goals and timetables" for the hiring of women and minorities. "The point of this pronouncement," wrote Harvard sociologist Nathan Glazer, was that "equal employment opportunity must now be redefined, against its plain meaning, not as opportunity, but result."[40] The era of "affirmative action" had begun.

The federal agency that played the biggest role in this evolution was the Equal Employment Opportunity Commission that, somewhat ironically, had been created by the Civil Rights Act of 1964 to enforce Title VII's hiring provisions. The act's statutory language and legislative history was clear. Racial hiring quotas were prohibited, and employers could be held liable only for "intentional" discrimination, not merely for the existence of statistical disparities in their workforce. The EEOC's professional staff, however, had its own ideas about what should constitute discrimination and viewed the statutory language as an obstacle to overcome rather than principles to defend. Alfred Blumrosen, an early EEOC administrator, would later acknowledge that the agency issued guidelines that in fact did not "flow from any clear congressional grant of authority" and that "required a reading of the statute contrary to the plain meaning."[41] He justified his actions on the grounds that intentional employment bias was too difficult to prove and that, in the interest of hastening black employment the EEOC should define "broadly" the discrimination proscribed under Title VII:

If discrimination is narrowly defined, for example, by requiring an evil intent to injure minorities, then it will be difficult to find that it exists. If it does not exist, then the plight of racial and ethnic minorities must be attributable to some more generalized failures in society, in the fields of basic education, housing, family relations, and the like. The search for efforts to improve the condition of minorities must then focus in these general and difficult areas, and the answers can come only gradually as basic institutions, attitudes, customs, and practices are changed.

But if discrimination is broadly defined, as, for example, by including all conduct which adversely affects minority group employment opportunities...then the prospects for rapid improvement in minority employment opportunities are greatly increased.[42]

At the center of the EEOC's legal strategy "was an attempt to build a body of case law in the lower federal courts that would replace the traditional intent test with an effects test," wrote Hugh Davis Graham. "This in turn would allow the agency to construct prima facie cases based on statistical data irrespective of intent, and through this device to throw upon employers a burden of proof that, in light of the damaging statistics, would be difficult to sustain."[43] The strategy paid off in 1971, when the Supreme Court endorsed the agency's redefinition of discrimination in *Griggs v. Duke Power Company*. The company had required workers to have a high school degree or pass an intelligence test to be hired or promoted to certain positions. Because disproportionate numbers of black applicants lacked a high school diploma or failed the test, the company was sued for racial discrimination. Even though Title VII authorized the use of ability tests so long as they weren't intentionally discriminatory, the court ruled unanimously for the plaintiffs that the company was guilty of employment discrimination because the results mattered more than intent. "*Griggs* shifted civil rights policy to a group-rights, equality-of-result rationale that made the social consequences of employment practices, rather than their purposes, intent, or motivation, the decisive consideration in determining their lawfulness," wrote legal historian Herman Belz. "The decision supplied a theoretical basis for preferential treatment as well as a practical incentive for extending race-conscious preference: employers' desire to avoid charges, based on racial imbalance, of discrimination."[44] The EEOC, with the support of the Supreme Court, had effectively turned Title VII on its head.

Just as *Brown* was reinterpreted by federal administrators and the courts to require taking race into account when assigning students to school, a statute intended to outlaw race-based hiring and promotion of workers was now reinterpreted to require color-conscious hiring and promotion. "The *Griggs* decision threw into doubt every employment practice having a 'disparate impact' upon minorities," wrote

journalist and author Terry Eastland. "Because of the potential liability, private employers now had to think about
whether or not the percentage of minorities working in their
companies mirrored the percentage of minorities in the area
labor force. *Griggs* created enormous pressure to hire and
promote by race and sex."[45]

Going forward, the court would continue to carve out
exceptions to the nondiscrimination principle at the heart
of the Civil Rights Act of 1964. Its seminal 1978 ruling in
Regents of the University of California v. Bakke sanctioned
the use of racial criteria to determine admission to colleges
and universities. A state medical school set aside admission
slots for black applicants. Allan Bakke, who was white, had
been rejected even though his grade point average and test
scores were far higher than the black students who had been
admitted. Title VI of the Civil Rights Act of 1964 states that
"No person in the United States shall, on the ground of race,
color, or national origin, be excluded from participation in,
be denied the benefits of, or be subjected to discrimination
under any program or activity receiving Federal financial assistance." Because the school received federal financial assistance, Bakke sued. Four members of the court agreed with
the plaintiff. Justice John Paul Stevens wrote that the statute's
language is "crystal clear: Race cannot be the basis of excluding anyone from a federally funded program." But four other
justices concluded that minority set-aside programs should
be permitted to address minority underrepresentation in the
medical profession. And a ninth justice, Lewis Powell, who

authored the controlling opinion for the court, determined that racial quotas were unconstitutional but that race could be used as a factor in admissions, so long as it wasn't the deciding factor and so long as the objective was to promote student diversity.

A 1979 decision by the court likewise ignored the plain text and legislative history of the Civil Rights Act of 1964 to advance what it considered a greater social good. In *United Steelworkers of America v. Weber*, the court permitted the use of overt racial quotas by an employer if they are "designed to break down old patterns of racial segregation and hierarchy." The plaintiff in the case, a white steelworker named Brian Weber, had attempted to join a training program sponsored by his employer and his union. The program admitted workers based on race, and Weber was rejected because he was white. Weber decided to sue his employer. Title VII of the Civil Rights Act of 1964 prohibited employers from classifying workers "in any way which would deprive or tend to deprive any individual of employment opportunities...because of such individual's race." Regarding Weber's complaint in particular, the statute also stipulated: "It shall be an unlawful employment practice for any employer, labor organization, or joint labor-management committee controlling apprenticeship or other training or retraining, including on-the-job training programs, to discriminate against any individual because of his race, color, religion, sex, or national origin in admission to, or employment in, any program established to provide apprenticeship or other training." Nevertheless,

Weber lost his case. The court acknowledged that its conclusion was inconsistent with the "literal" language of Title VII and instead relied on the "spirit" of the statute.

In the 1950s, civil rights advocates focused on advancing equal treatment for individuals regardless of race, a notion that enjoyed broad and growing public support. By the end of the 1970s, the focus was on racial favoritism for certain groups, which was broadly unpopular and racially divisive. Activists, bureaucrats, and the judiciary were rejecting color blindness that the Constitution and legislation demanded and, under the banner of "affirmative action," creating a racial spoils system in a country that was rapidly becoming more racially and ethnically diverse. Moreover, this was being done in the name of helping the black underclass. The following chapters will explore the track record of these efforts.

THREE

Before Affirmative Action

A History of Accomplishment

Derrick Bell is best known today for his contributions to critical race theory, which posits that racism stems not only from individuals but is also embedded in American law and institutions, and that the historical mistreatment of black people largely explains current social and economic disparities. Critical race theorists have adopted the Marxian template, replacing class with race. Where Marxist theory emphasizes an economic power struggle based on class, in which capitalists benefit only through exploiting workers, critical race theory maintains that whites advance by exploiting blacks and other ethnic minority groups.

Before becoming the first black tenured professor at Harvard Law School in the 1970s, Bell had been a lawyer for the NAACP Legal Defense and Education Fund, where he worked on school desegregation cases under the tutelage of Thurgood Marshall. Over time, however, he grew unhappy with the pace of black progress and came to believe that racism is so deeply embedded in our society that color-blind remedies were destined to fail. By the mid-1980s, Bell, who died in 2011, was calling progress in race relations "largely a mirage, obscuring the fact that whites continue, consciously or unconsciously, to do all in their power to ensure their dominion and maintain their control" over blacks.[1] "Black people will never gain full equality in this country," he wrote in his 1992 book, *Faces at the Bottom of the Well*. "Even those herculean efforts we hail as successful will produce no more than temporary 'peaks of progress,' short-lived victories that slide into irrelevance as racial patterns adapt in ways that maintain white dominance. This is a hard-to-accept fact that all history verifies."[2]

One irony is that Bell, who in his later years became a fierce advocate of racial favoritism for blacks in higher education, had once been a critic of the practice. Following the assassination of Martin Luther King Jr. in 1968 and the unrest that ensued nationwide, including on college campuses, schools stepped up efforts to recruit black students and faculty. "In that time, there was a sense, pure and simple, that universities had to do their part to help integrate higher education," said Lee Bollinger, who was a law student at Columbia University in the late 1960s and later became president of the school.[3] To expedite the push for more racial diversity, elite colleges also began lowering their admissions and hiring standards. Previous black recruitment efforts had involved searching for capable students who already met existing admission criteria and could handle the academic rigor of a prestige institution. Now, for the first time, these schools were creating special programs to recruit black students with known academic deficiencies. How these underqualified recruits would fare once enrolled apparently was far less important to college administrators than upping the number of black faces on campus as quickly as possible. The haste in which schools proceeded, however, came at a high cost to the black "beneficiaries." Studies conducted in the late 1960s and early 1970s showed, predictably, that at some elite schools fully half of undergraduates admitted through special programs for blacks were on academic probation.[4]

In a 1970 law review article, "Black Students in White Law Schools," Bell objected to this new trend of using different criteria to assess student performance based on race and ethnic background. In the past, he noted, the small percentages of blacks admitted to the more-selective white law schools "not only met the usual academic criteria, but were often characterized by a strong inner drive to equal and, if at all possible, excel their white classmates."[5] The difference in the quality of black students now being admitted for appearances, Bell wrote, was "monumental." However well-intentioned, it was condescending and unhelpful to ask less of black people. "The view that black students, by reason of their deprived background and racist experiences, should not be required to perform as regular law students," he noted, "is a form of benevolent paternalism" that feeds racist stereotypes among whites and takes a psychic toll on blacks. "[W]hat does such a seemingly sympathetic policy do to the black student's self-esteem?" he asked.[6]

Bell further argued that racial double standards deceived black students by implicitly telling them that they should expect the same academic results as their white peers without trying as hard. "It is not that the blacks will be handicapped by the necessity of competing with whites, but that they are, by reason of the altered admissions criteria, denied the signal of their competence which students admitted under traditional qualifications receive," Bell observed.[7] He called on schools to offer black students "a more realistic appraisal" of their talents, potential, and likelihood of success at these institutions while still applying "no less demanding standards."[8] Finally, Bell warned that racial preferences ran the risk of tainting the accomplishments—in the eyes of whites and blacks alike—of those blacks who did manage to succeed. "Whatever arguments are used to justify such a policy, there is little denying that it robs those black students who have done well of receiving real credit and the boost in confidence that their accomplishments merit."[9] He referenced the "growing tide of bitterness and resentment" toward these practices and insisted that in "judging the work of black students, there is no reason to apply criteria more stringent than those used to judge whites, and no excuse for passing blacks on lower standards."[10]

Again, Derrick Bell would in later decades change his perspective on the utility of affirmative action policies, but there is no reason to think that his earlier views were insincere. In hindsight, Bell offered a preview of a half-century of arguments that would be made against racial preferences. He was hardly the only scholar to recognize the shortcomings of these policies, but the fact that the criticism came from Bell, someone who had dedicated his professional career to advancing the interests of fellow blacks, might give pause to those who are inclined to dismiss criticism of affirmative action as racist.

Bell's concerns about the psychological toll that these policies would take on black America turned out to be especially prescient. Five decades of affirmative action has given many people the false impression that black advancement is inextricably linked to special treatment in the form of ethnic preferences. In anticipation of the Supreme Court's 2023 ruling against racial preferences in *Students for Fair Admissions v. Harvard*, the *Chronicle of Higher Education* published a special "diversity" issue with a cover that read, "After Affirmative Action: The Imperiled Future of Race-Conscious Admissions." Alas, there was almost no diversity of opinion offered on the merits of affirmative action, which the editors deemed an unalloyed good. The only thing worth debating, as the *Chronicle* saw matters, was whether we wanted to live in a society that "clings to the ideal of color blindness at all costs, or one that recognizes the continuing struggle of integration." After all, doesn't America's "long history of white supremacy" make "race-based affirmative action necessary"? And isn't affirmative action little more than "a modest gesture in the direction of racial justice"?[11]

The *Chronicle* was representative of the elite left's dire view of a post–affirmative action society. Noah Feldman, a Harvard law professor, said that striking down race-conscious admissions policies meant colleges "would no longer be allowed to pursue racial diversity."[12] And Sherrilyn Ifill, a former head of the NAACP Legal Defense Fund, said that court-imposed "race neutrality" would have "catastrophic implications" for blacks.[13] Paul Butler, a law professor at Georgetown University, went even further. "I can't imagine teaching stop-and-frisk without Black male students to talk about what it's like to experience that humiliation in the real world," he wrote. "But I'd better get used to it if I continue to teach at institutions that will soon stop admitting people who look like me. The Supreme Court's inevitable decision will have immediate and catastrophic consequences. Public and private universities will resegregate."[14]

This doomsaying rests mainly on the assumption that racial favoritism is a prerequisite for black advancement in a country where anti-black racism still exists. Because it has been asserted so many times and for so many decades that affirmative action and other government programs are responsible for the existence of today's black middle class, few people bother to question the veracity of this claim. Yet whether black people have advanced more under quotas and set-asides than under non-preferential policies is ultimately an empirical question, even if it is seldom analyzed empirically. Instead, there is a tendency to focus on black suffering and downplay black accomplishment. But black history is about more than victimization at the hands of whites.

"It will not do," observed the scholar John McWhorter, "to render black history as a succession of tragedies: the horrors of slavery, Dred Scott, the quick demise of Reconstruction, *Plessy v. Ferguson*, the rise of the Ku Klux Klan, lynchings, the beating of Civil Rights activists, Emmett Till. To not attend to such things at all would be folly of course. But even so, a history dominated by such horrors is not one to exactly inspire us for the future."[15] During the first two-thirds of the twentieth century, well before affirmative action and an expanded welfare state supposedly came to the rescue, black people experienced significant progress. Education gaps narrowed, incomes rose, and poverty declined. This history hasn't received the attention it deserves because black politicians and activists have a vested interest in a narrative that accentuates black suffering. The upshot is that a history of social and economic advancement that should be a source of pride for blacks—and a source of inspiration for other ethnic minority groups—has received relatively little consideration.

One of the earliest comprehensive assessments of black progress after slavery came from Monroe Work, a sociologist and director of research at Booker T. Washington's Tuskegee Institute in Alabama. Work's *Negro Yearbook*, first published in 1912, documented, among other things, black literacy rates, property ownership, and business formation. The 1913 edition marked the fiftieth anniversary of the Emancipation Proclamation and boasted that "no other emancipated people have made so great a progress in so short a time." Comparing former slaves in the United States to former serfs in Russia, the *Yearbook* noted:

> The Russian serfs were emancipated in 1861. Fifty years after it was found that 14,000,000 of them had accumulated about $500,000,000 worth of property or about $36 per capita, an average of about $200 per family. Fifty years after their emancipation only about 30 percent of the Russian peasants were able to read and write. After fifty years of freedom the ten million Negroes in the United States have accumulated over $700,000,000 worth of property, or about $70 per capita, which is an average of $350 per family. After fifty years of freedom 70 percent of them have some education in books.[16]

Black advancement in education predates the end of slavery and government assistance. While the overwhelming majority of blacks living in the antebellum period were enslaved, a small percentage were legally free. From 1800 to

1860 these "free persons of color" averaged between 10 percent and 14 percent of the nation's total black population. According to census data, there were 434,000 free blacks in 1850, and an estimated 59 percent of them were able to read and write, even though they were barred from attending public schools in most Northern cities as well as in the South.[17] To educate their children, blacks set up private schools, some of which were operated in secret, and private instruction would play an essential role in black schooling well into the twentieth century.

"In 15 out of 16 cities with large free Negro populations in 1850, all but one had more literate than illiterate 'free persons of color,'" one study of the period noted. "These included Deep South cities like Mobile, Savannah, and New Orleans. In Savannah, no Negroes were reported as attending school anywhere in the county, and yet the number of illiterate free Negroes in the county was less than one-third the free Negro population of Savannah alone."[18] It wasn't until 1916 that the number of blacks attending public high schools in the US was as high as the number attending private high schools.[19] Those who argue today against parental school choice on the grounds that low-income families lack the knowledge or wherewithal to look out for their kids' educational interests, either don't know this history or willfully ignore it.

Of course, most black Americans are not descendants of "free persons of color" but rather the progeny of four million black people who were enslaved before the Civil War. Data collected by the Freedmen's Bureau, the federal government agency that was tasked with assisting former slaves, offers insight into the priorities of the newly freed black population. Prior to the war, every Southern state except Tennessee prohibited teaching slaves to read, and as of 1860 more than 90 percent of black adults in the South were illiterate.[20] By 1870, however, about 20 percent of blacks over the age of nine could read and write. "Perhaps the most striking illustration of the freedmen's quest for self-improvement was their seemingly unquenchable thirst for education," wrote historian Eric Foner. "Northern benevolent societies, the Freedmen's Bureau, and, after 1868, state governments, provided most of the funding for black education during Reconstruction. But the initiative often lay with blacks themselves, a pattern established in the early days of the war." In the Civil War's aftermath, Freedmen's Bureau officials "repeatedly expressed surprise at discovering classes organized by blacks already meeting in churches, basements, or private homes," Foner noted. "By the end of 1865, less than a month after Union troops occupied the city, over 1,000 black children and seventy-five adults attended schools established by Richmond's black churches and the American Missionary Association."[21] With the assistance of the Freedmen's Bureau, nearly four thousand schools for blacks were established by the end of 1866. A decade later, more than half of white children and roughly 40 percent of black children attended schools.[22]

In 1877, federal troops left the South, ending Reconstruction and ushering in a new era of white supremacy that would manifest itself in racial intimidation, legal segregation, and black voter disenfranchisement. Education opportunities were reduced by gerrymandered school districts designed to steer tax dollars away from black communities. One analysis of the post-Reconstruction period found that the "disparity between black and white public schools in per capita expenditures was greater in 1910 than in 1900 in every southern state."[23] And resources weren't the only challenge that black schools faced. One historian, citing a *New York Times* article from the period, noted that in "the 10 years since the end of the war, hundreds of new black schools had been burned across the South, dozens of teachers terrorized and killed."[24] In the 1890s, the number of lynchings in the South averaged more than one hundred per year. Nevertheless, the 1910 census reported a black literacy rate of 70 percent. It's conceivable that some respondents may have exaggerated their reading and writing capabilities to census takers, according to economic historian Robert Higgs. "But even if the true literacy figure a half century after emancipation reached only 50 percent, the magnitude of the accomplishment is still striking, especially when one recalls the overwhelming obstacles blocking black educational efforts," he observed. "For a large population to transform itself from virtually unlettered to more than half literate in 50 years ranks as an accomplishment seldom witnessed in human history."[25]

Given the hostile conditions in the South, black educators such as Booker T. Washington turned to Northern philanthropists for assistance. These included John D. Rockefeller, Andrew Carnegie, and the Chicago-based Julius Rosenwald, who made his fortune as head of retail giant Sears, Roebuck and Company. Between 1914 and 1932, the Rosenwald matching-grant program, created to address racial learning gaps in the South, would contribute to the construction of nearly five thousand schools with combined seating capacity for more than 660,000 students across fifteen states. The Rosenwald schools were superior to what came before them in just about every way. The buildings were sturdier and had better lighting and ventilation. Classrooms were equipped with books, chairs, desks, and blackboards. Teachers received better training and higher pay.

An analysis of the Washington-Rosenwald alliance was published by the Federal Reserve Bank of Chicago in 2011. The authors noted that blacks born in the South between 1880 and 1910 had completed three fewer years of schooling than white Southerners. Both groups had made absolute gains over that period, but blacks had experienced no relative progress. Thanks to the Rosenwald initiative, however, both the quality of black education and the percentage of black children attending school would improve dramatically. "Within a generation, the racial gap in the South declined to well under a year and was comparable in size to the racial gap in the North," the authors concluded. "Our main finding is that rural Black students with access to Rosenwald schools completed over a full year more education than Black students with no access to Rosenwald schools, a magnitude that, in the aggregate, explains close to 40 percent of the observed Black-White convergence in educational attainment in the South for cohorts born between 1910 and 1925."[26] Today, defenders of affirmative action argue that the policy is needed to assure racial diversity in schools, which they consider essential to narrowing the achievement gap. And critics accuse charter schools that cater to low-income minority students—and often receive financial support from titans of industry—of promoting segregated learning. Yet even in the Jim Crow era, black students needed access to quality schools more than they needed access to white classmates.

As discussed earlier, blacks began leaving the rural South in large numbers in the 1910s. The migration was triggered by World War I, which reduced European immigration and increased the demand for factory workers. Some blacks headed to cities in the South, but many more fled to the urban North, where there was a wider variety of industrial jobs with higher pay. In the 1920s this migration doubled, before slowing somewhat during the Great Depression. At the onset of World War II, however, a second and even larger migration of blacks out of the South began. When it finally petered out in the 1960s, the demographic profile of blacks looked significantly different, both socially and economically. It wasn't merely that blacks made progress during this period—indeed, all groups progressed. What's significant is that the black population *gained ground* on the white population by many important measures. Black-white gaps narrowed substantially in everything from poverty and income to schooling and homeownership, and all of this occurred well before the affirmative action era.

Economist Leah Platt Boustan found that "southern blacks could have expected to more than double their earnings by moving to the North as of 1940," compared to the 50 percent pay hike that Southern white migrants could have anticipated. She added: "Even after adjusting for the fact that migrants may have had higher earnings potential, I find that movers earned twice as much as those who stayed behind. Indeed, almost upon first arrival, black migrants earned on parity with northern-born blacks in the northern economy."[27] In 1920, the farmhand in rural Alabama earning 75 cents per day, and the industrial worker in Birmingham earning $2.50 per day, could head to Milwaukee or Chicago and find work that paid between $3.20 and $4.80 per day. "Southern blacks who were able to move directly from agricultural labor to an industrial occupation in the North may have increased their earnings by as much as 300 percent," according to Boustan.[28]

The progress was undeniable, but it was also uneven. In Milwaukee, for example, the number of blacks engaged in professional, business, and clerical work was quite small in absolute numbers—increasing from 80 in 1910 to 301 in 1930—but it grew by more than 120 percent in the 1920s alone, which was faster than it rose among the city's overall population. And even though, according to one study, black women "acquired more clerical positions than did men during the 1920s, these pursuits constituted the lowest percentage (3.2) of black women in the labor force."[29] A history of Chicago's black Bronzeville neighborhood noted that as of 1938, blacks owned and operated some 2,600 businesses, though most "were small retail stores and service enterprises on side streets, or in the older, less desirable communities."[30] A 1947 census bureau study of New York City, however, showed "record numbers" of black New Yorkers, including women, moving out of service positions. "There was a marked shift among employed Black women away from domestic labor and into clerical, sales, and semi-skilled jobs: 64 percent were domestics in 1940, while only 36 percent were so employed in 1947," the survey found. "There was also a sharp drop in service work for men, from 40 percent so employed in 1940 to 23 percent in 1947. From 1940 to 1944 the proportion of Black workers in skilled or semi-skilled positions had doubled. The biggest shift was out of personal service and into semi-skilled jobs."[31]

Much of this progress occurred in the private sector, even though racial discrimination was legal. Blacks may have been a disfavored group, but a free-market economy can exact a price on bigoted employers. A businessowner who is unwilling to hire black workers or pay them the same wages as equally productive white employees could risk losing profits and market share to less-prejudiced competitors who hire the most qualified applicants regardless of race. Discrimination thus becomes an added cost of doing business, and many employers don't want to pay that added cost. Economic self-interest doesn't eliminate racism, but it can reduce the incentive to discriminate. However, the hiring of blacks in government or in noncompetitive markets (colleges, hospitals, regulated utilities), where there are no economic profits to forgo, was another matter entirely. There, blacks continued to struggle, and Uncle Sam was one of the worst offenders. A black labor leader in the 1940s called the US government "the nation's biggest Jim Crow employer." A 1947 *New York Times* article, wrote historian Martha Biondi, "identified fourteen federal departments that practiced racial discrimination, and overall, Black federal employees were assigned the most menial, lowest-paying jobs regardless of their education or qualifications."[32]

Yet even if there had been less racial intolerance during this period, blacks were not qualified for many of the better-paying jobs, which makes it difficult to determine with any precision how much of a role racism played in the black-white earnings gap compared to other factors. As a group, blacks lagged whites significantly in schooling, both quantitatively and qualitatively. Even those blacks who had received some education before leaving the South had likely attended inferior elementary and secondary schools. That dynamic would change for the better in the ensuing decades and eventually begin to manifest itself in higher-paying jobs and lower rates of black poverty—even as the racial oppression of Jim Crow continued. A 1978 Rand Corporation study reported that in 1920, black children attended school only about two-thirds as many days as white children, yet by 1954 this black-white disparity had all but disappeared. Similarly, it noted that "in 1920 teachers of black students had one and three-fourths as many pupils as the average teacher in the country. By 1954, this difference had been substantially reduced."[33] In 1940, whites between the ages of twenty-five and twenty-nine had 3.6 years more schooling than their black counterparts. By 1960, both groups had advanced but blacks outpaced whites, and the gap narrowed by more than half to 1.7 years. Most white-collar jobs, then as now, require a high school degree. Between 1940 and 1960, the percentage of blacks who met that qualification would more than triple, once again growing at a much faster rate than the increase among whites.[34]

Progress also occurred in the South, where racial oppression was most acute and where a majority of the black population in the US still resided even after the large-scale migrations that started during World War I and intensified during World War II. "By 1960 Southern high school attendance rates were at 82 percent for whites and 69 percent for blacks," wrote Robert Putnam and Shaylyn Romney Garrett in their 2020 book, *The Upswing*. More high school attendance begat more college attendance, and the authors also noted the sharp uptick among black college students in the South in the first half of the twentieth century, "from 2,168 enrolled in college in 1900 to 29,269 in 1935, to 63,000 in 1952." At the time, the vast majority of blacks who pursued higher education attended historically black colleges. Between 1940 and 1950, enrollment at these institutions grew from 43,000 to more than 76,000, a 56 percent increase. Obviously, blacks didn't *need* racial preferences to attend college because there were none. What they did need was money, which was provided via the GI Bill for veterans returning from World War II. In 1947, the number of veterans attending predominantly white colleges and universities grew by 29 percent. At black colleges, it grew by 50 percent.[35]

Beginning in the late 1960s, more white colleges would open their campuses to blacks, and black college attendance would continue to rise. "In 1950, 50,000 blacks had graduated from college, most at historically black institutions," wrote journalist Bob Zelnick. "By 1960, the number had reached 200,000; by 1970, 470,000, more than half from integrated colleges and universities."[36] Also in the late 1960s, however, more white colleges began compromising their admission standards to admit black students with weaker academic credentials who otherwise would not have made the cut. The negative consequences of doing so became evident almost immediately. According to the scholars Putnam and Romney Garrett, education gaps that had been narrowing started to widen. Greater numbers of blacks had been graduating from high school and entering college, but now fewer were completing college relative to their white peers. The "fastest and most dramatic progress toward parity between blacks and whites finishing high school was achieved before 1970," the authors wrote in 2020. "But after 1970, the relative rate at which blacks were completing college dropped, then flatlined, and never recovered its previous upward trajectory. In fact, today black Americans are completing college at a lower rate compared to whites than they were in 1970."[37]

In her dissenting opinion in *Students for Fair Admissions v. Harvard*, which barred race-conscious college admissions,

Justice Sonia Sotomayor wrote that the majority opinion "rolls back decades of precedent and momentous progress." In a separate dissent, Justice Ketanji Brown Jackson said the majority ruling had "detached itself from this country's actual past and present experience." Yet actual past experience clearly shows that black advancement in higher education was far more momentous in the decades immediately prior to the implementation of quotas and set-asides. In fact, the advent of racial preferences coincided with the end of a black-white convergence in the quantity and quality of education in the US that had been occurring for nearly a century. Why trends in black college enrollment changed for the worse will be discussed in later chapters. The point to note here is that well before the implementation of racial preference policies, blacks were making unprecedented strides despite facing tremendous racial hostility. Those who credit affirmative action with black educational advancement are getting the order wrong. The black advancement came first.

A similar story can be told with respect to black incomes. More education meant better jobs, which in turn meant higher pay. And just as absolute and relative educational gains among blacks had been speedier in the decades prior to racial preferences in college admissions, wages for black workers rose at a faster pace in the decades before racial hiring quotas became commonplace. Once again, this is an area where affirmative action policies have received far more credit than they warrant, mainly because proponents get the sequence wrong or start the story in the middle. In 1939, the annual median income was $360 for black males and $1,112 for white males. By 1960 those median incomes had reached $3,075 and $5,137, respectively, representing a 568 percent increase for blacks versus a 362 percent increase for whites. Among females over the same time period, there was a 275 percent increase among whites and a significantly higher 418 percent increase among blacks.[38] And all of this occurred not only before affirmative action but also prior to the major civil rights legislation of the mid-1960s.

Between 1940 and 1970, median annual incomes for black men rose from 41 percent of what white men were earning to 59 percent, an 18-point gain. Yet under the first quarter-century of affirmative action policies, from 1970 to 1995, black male earnings as a percentage of white earnings grew by just 8 more points, to 67 percent. Among black women, the pre–affirmative action gains were even more dramatic. Median black female earnings climbed from 36 percent of what white women earned in 1940 to 73 percent by 1970. Between 1970 and 1995, however, pay for black women grew by only 16 more points.[39] Black earnings clearly were rising at a much faster pace in the decades prior to the 1970s—the first full decade of affirmative action. They continued to rise thereafter, but more slowly. To say that affirmative action led to the jump in black incomes is to willfully ignore the preexisting trendlines. At best, racial preferences helped to continue something that was already happening. At worst, racial preferences did more to throttle than to expedite black upward mobility. When proponents of race-preferences trumpet the income gains of blacks since 1970, they misleadingly start the story in the middle.

During the 1960s, black family income doubled while white family income rose by only 69 percent. Outside of the South as far back as 1959, black married couples earned 78 percent of what their white counterparts earned, and by 1971 that number had grown to 93 percent.[40] According to economist Richard Vedder, black wage gains historically have correlated with neither racial preferences nor large expansions of the welfare state, such as the implementation of President Lyndon Johnson's War on Poverty initiatives. "Before 1960, the typical (median) black had slightly less than one-half the income of whites," Vedder noted in a 2021 academic paper. "That proportion rose sharply to about 70 percent by around 1970, when it stagnated to the early 1990s, at which point it rose again to about 80 percent at the beginning of the twenty-first century, where it has been ever since." The author found it especially noteworthy that "the gains in the 1960s were observed largely before the vast expansion of the welfare state and that the increases in the 1990s came in a period when some forms of public assistance were rolled back in the Personal Responsibility and Work Opportunity Reconciliation Act of 1996, which put lifelong time limits on receipt of public assistance and installed some work requirements." The watering down of 1990s welfare reform policies over the past two decades—expanding eligibility and reducing work requirements, for example—"has likely stalled again the move toward racial income equality."[41]

This higher pay reflected better jobs as millions of blacks entered middle-class occupations. In 1940, 43 percent of black men worked in agriculture, typically as low-wage sharecroppers or farm laborers, but by 1960 just 14 percent of black men were still engaged in such work. "Conversely, in 1940 only one out of ten black men had any kind of white-collar or skilled manual job, a rough but reasonably good indicator of what it means to be 'middle class,'" according to one history of the period. "The proportions of African-American men working as factory operatives almost doubled in these years as well, rising from 13 to 24 percent." Some 60 percent of black women who worked in 1940 were domestic servants, but by 1960 that number had been cut nearly in half as black women moved into jobs as factory workers, clerks, and schoolteachers.[42] In the 1950s, New York City had the largest urban black population in the country. "The signs of Negro prosperity are everywhere," wrote *Time* magazine in 1953. "On the rooftops of Manhattan's Harlem grows the bare, ugly forest of TV antennae which has become a new symbol of middle-class achievement," the article added. "There are signs that the Negro has begun to develop a large, strong middle class." The scholar Michael Javen Fortner reported that in 1950s New York City, the number of black engineers increased by 134 percent, and the number of black schoolteachers grew by 125 percent. The ranks of black physicians, lawyers, nurses, and social workers grew by 56 percent, 55 percent, 90 percent, and 146 percent, respectively.[43] "The proportion of white-collar workers in Harlem increased from 34.1 percent in 1950 to 36.9 percent in 1960, then to 46 percent in 1970," Fortner wrote. "At the same time, the proportion of blue-collar workers decreased from 38.9 percent in 1950 to 37 percent in 1960, then to 29.5 percent in 1970."[44]

Worth noting is that the *Time* magazine article was reporting on trends that predated the 1954 landmark *Brown v. Board of Education* decision, never mind the Civil Rights Act of 1964 and the Voting Rights Act of 1965. There is no intention here to downplay the significance of court rulings and legislation that made America more just, or to diminish the sacrifices of civil rights activists who fought for racial equality. At the same time, the record shows that black progress was not dependent or in any way conditioned on those events. The takeaway is that the elimination of white racism, however desirable then and now, is not a prerequisite for black socioeconomic advancement. Racial gaps in the twenty-first century are regularly blamed on racism or the legacy of slavery and segregation. But there was no shortage of racism in the 1940s and '50s, when racial gaps were narrowing by almost every significant measure. Logic suggests that any subsequent retrogression among blacks has been due primarily to factors other than racism, structural or otherwise, yet racial animus continues to be mindlessly cited by liberal public intellectuals, journalists, activists, and others as an all-purpose explanation for social and economic racial disparities.

What was happening in pre–affirmative action New York City was happening, to various degrees, in other parts of the country. Nationwide, between 1960 and 1970 the number of black male accountants, foremen, welders, and police officers grew by between 68 percent (accountants) and 152 percent (foremen). Between 1960 and 1972, the number of blacks categorized as "white collar workers," "craftsmen," and "operatives" grew from 2.9 million to 5.1 million, or by 75 percent. The increase among comparable whites during the same decade was only 23 percent.[45] More education and higher pay led to tremendous reductions in black poverty—well before civil rights laws, an expanded welfare state, and affirmative action policies would come along and be given much of the credit. "While the African American middle class was expanding, the proportion of blacks stuck on the very bottom rung of the social ladder was shrinking," according to the scholars Stephan and Abigail Thernstrom. "The 1940s and 1950s saw a striking decline in black poverty, well before the federal government launched a War on Poverty, outlawed discrimination in employment, and mandated affirmative action in employment and education."[46] In 1940, some four-fifths of black families (87 percent) were impoverished. By 1960, it was fewer than half (47 percent). During the 1960s it fell to 30 percent, but during the first two decades of affirmative action—1970 to 1990—black poverty declined by just one percentage point.[47]

Richard Vedder calculated that the "greatest twenty-five years of black progress after Emancipation itself" came between 1948 and 1973, when the median income of the black population doubled. During this period, "black incomes rose from 45.3 to 70.1 percent of white incomes, eliminating nearly half the income disparity between the two races."[48]

Robert Putnam and Shaylyn Romney Garrett reported similar findings. "[M]ost scholars agree that income levels by race converged at the greatest rate between 1940 and 1970," they wrote. "The very same factors that were creating income equalization across the American economy at this time were also driving equalization between white and black workers, especially as black workers moved to places where they could access better jobs. In fact, far from leaving African Americans out, the Great Convergence disproportionately benefited them."[49] Racial preferences are credited with advancing blacks, but it would be more accurate to say that the implementation of affirmative action policies in the 1970s coincided with a period of black stagnation. Previous progress in the 1940s, '50s, and '60s slowed down or stalled beginning in the 1970s. The black-white disparity in family income in 2018 was approximately where it was in 1968.[50] Many are quick to blame the legacy of slavery or Jim Crow for that statistic, but what about the legacy of government programs in general and racial preferences in particular? Under policies promoting equal treatment, America's black population rose significantly, both in absolute terms and relative to whites. Under policies promoting special treatment, those gains leveled off. On balance, blacks have fared better under color-blind policies than they have under policies that promoted racial discrimination or racial favoritism.

These facts are too often glossed over or ignored entirely in discussions about the effectiveness of policies that pick winners and losers based on race. On balance, racial preferences have been ineffective in helping the most disadvantaged black Americans. Affirmative action has slowed whatever previous black progress was already occurring, while giving blacks and whites alike the impression that black people are charity cases dependent on government programs. The reality is that black people essentially lifted themselves out of poverty in the first two-thirds of the twentieth century—before affirmative action. They owe their rise to hard work, not special treatment. The tragedy is that what should be a point of pride among blacks—an odds-defying rise in America unmatched by any racial or ethnic group in history—is often downplayed in the media when it's mentioned at all. Worse, blacks and whites alike have been led to believe that black people can't advance without racial preferences, even though there is a long history in this country of them doing exactly that.

If you are someone who believes that anti-black bias in America is systemic, however, and must be eliminated root and branch before any significant narrowing of racial disparities can take place, this record of accomplishment is problematic. You downplay or dismiss these hard facts because they undermine—and may even refute entirely—your claims about the main causes of racial inequality today and how best to address them based on past experience. And if you are a black intellectual or political leader who supports racial double standards, this history of black upward mobility risks exposing you as a hypocrite, which is the type of criticism that

Derrick Bell faced after he himself shifted from an affirmative action skeptic to an advocate.

"Bell is a law professor and legal scholar whose work is either praised in public or dismissed as mediocre in private, dependent on whether the occasion is one demanding convention or is safe enough to allow honesty to take on the invisible form of words spoken off the record," wrote the black social critic Stanley Crouch in the early 1990s. "Bell's reputation has been built upon squawking about the supposed inevitability of racism. According to him, black Americans will never get a fair chance because the racist tattoo on the white sensibility is irremovable." Crouch wrote that Bell's own career trajectory would seem to undermine the argument that racism and discrimination weren't decreasing and that blacks can't advance due to systemic oppression. "I accuse Bell and his ilk of being, fundamentally, defeatists, people who accept high positions of success, then tell those below them that *they* don't have a chance," he wrote. "Pay no attention to *me*: the white man wouldn't budge for *you*."[51]

The racial essentialism at the heart of critical race theory has gained a much wider audience more recently thanks to social justice advocates such as Michelle Alexander, Ta-Nehisi Coates, Robin DiAngelo, and Ibram X. Kendi. Their widely discussed essays and best-selling books have plenty to say about systemic racism, white privilege, and unconscious bias but have next to nothing to say about what blacks have nonetheless achieved. Today, the false assumptions and racial resentment that animate critical race theory can be found in

K–12 classrooms via the *New York Times* 1619 Project, and they have entered the workplace through consultants hired to conduct diversity and racial sensitivity training. Alexander rose to prominence after publishing *The New Jim Crow*, a polemic about racial disparities in incarceration rates that all but ignored racial disparities in crime rates, as if the two phenomena have nothing to do with one another. The writings of Ta-Nehisi Coates, as will be discussed in the following chapter, argue in favor of slavery reparations but present no empirical evidence that what currently ails the black poor can be addressed by allowing them to cash in on the exploitation of dead ancestors.

"White identity is inherently racist; white people do not exist outside the system of white supremacy," according to DiAngelo, a prominent author and proselytizer of critical race thinking. "I strive to be 'less white.' To be less white is to be less racially oppressive."[52] During a visit in 2023 to a middle school in Durham, North Carolina, Kendi told an assembly of eighth graders: "If a particular group is richer than another group, it's not because they're better; it's because bad rules—racist rules—allowed them to get those riches."[53] In his *New York Times* bestseller, *How to Be an Antiracist*, Kendi openly embraced racial discrimination against white people. "The only remedy to racist discrimination is antiracist discrimination," he wrote. "The only remedy to past discrimination is present discrimination. The only remedy to present discrimination is future discrimination."[54] The "language of color blindness," he wrote, "is a mask to hide when someone is being racist." For Kendi, "a color-blind Constitution" simply perpetuates "a White-supremacist America."[55]

As the writings of DiAngelo, Kendi, and others suggest, critical race theory amounts to little more than a fancy justification for racial favoritism, and it always has. In a lengthy 1989 *Harvard Law Review* article, Randall Kennedy, a black law professor, challenged the rationalizations used by Derrick Bell and other prominent critical race theorists to push for reverse discrimination. Kennedy detailed the "empirical weakness" of their arguments, accused advocates of " 'crying wolf' too casually," and noted the "strategic use of accusations of prejudice" to advance their ideology.[56] Critical race theorists, he wrote, trafficked in backward notions of race and destiny to make a self-serving case that the ethnicity of certain minorities should automatically serve as an intellectual credential in academic hiring and promotion. To Kennedy, credentializing racial status was unprincipled opportunism and simply didn't pass the smell test:

> One hears that there is a need to consult the racial identity of candidates...for faculty positions in order to attain a given racial perspective—for example, "a black perspective" or, as it is frequently stated, "the black perspective." But what makes a perspective or opinion or style "black"? What constitutes a "black" perspective, for instance, in a debate over affirmative action where the antagonists are themselves blacks? If all the antagonists

are deemed to voice black perspectives simply because they are black, the term "black perspective"
would seem to have only a circular, tautological
character: a black perspective is a perspective articulated by a black....

None of the contributors to the racial critique
literature who have articulated what I have called
the racial distinctiveness thesis have offered a substantive definition of blackness. This is unsurpris-
ing, for such a definition would pose difficulties
for them. Their claim of racial distinctiveness accentuates commonality among scholars of color
and difference between them and white scholars.
But given the reality of intra-racial disagreement
and interracial crossover, a substantive definition of blackness would give rise to a situation in
which an appreciable number of white intellectuals would be deemed to espouse "black" points of
view.[57]

Toward the end of his essay, Kennedy revealed that black
colleagues who had read earlier drafts urged him not to air
his criticism of critical race advocates out of concern that it
would undermine their arguments for racial preferences. To
his credit, he ignored them. "I have been advised—in some
instances warned—to forgo publishing this Article because,
among other things, it will be put to bad use by enemies of racial justice," he wrote. Some critics argue "that my comments

on racial distinctiveness claims are hostile to affirmative action insofar as they throw into doubt certain ideas that have been mobilized in favor of racial preferences in faculty hiring, particularly the notion that race should serve as a positive intellectual credential for minority scholars."[58]

In a 2021 collection of essays, Kennedy wrote that Derrick Bell was among those who implored him not to publish the law review article, "believing that those hostile to CRT would wield my assessment 'as a club to denigrate and even deny tenure to young scholars who dared identify with the new movement.' "[59] Bell, like advocates of racial preferences today, claimed to be speaking on behalf of the black poor while in fact he was speaking on behalf of himself and other already better-off blacks who stood to benefit the most from special treatment. The goal was not to abolish racist policies per se but rather to change who's on the receiving end.

FOUR

The Reparations Ruckus

Cents and Nonsense

While campaigning for president in 2019, Senator Elizabeth Warren told a town hall audience in Jackson, Mississippi, that "it's time to start the national, full-blown conversation about reparations." Other progressives seeking the Democratic presidential nomination at the time, including Senators Kamala Harris and Cory Booker, also had endorsed proposals to compensate black descendants of slaves. Contrary to what Warren implied, however, slavery reparations had been a subject of intense discussion for decades. What had changed more recently was not the willingness to talk about reparations but rather the level of open support for it among prominent Democratic officials and others who endorse racial favoritism.

Like affirmative action, "antiracism," and various "diversity, equity, and inclusion" schemes, reparations is another means of offering preferential treatment based on racial heritage. And like critical race theory, it is an idea that has moved from the fringe to the mainstream in recent years. Barack Obama opposed reparations when he ran for president in 2008, as did Hillary Clinton and Bernie Sanders eight years later. Back then, it was a fixation of black nationalists and others on the political far left but shunned by most liberal Democrats. In the late 1960s, the political activist James Forman released a Black Manifesto demanding $500 million from "white Christian churches and Jewish synagogues" for "reparations due us as people who have been exploited and degraded, brutalized, killed and persecuted."[1] But no major civil rights organizations aligned themselves with Forman, who raised only a few hundred thousand dollars before the effort petered out. Jesse Jackson called for reparations in a speech to black activists in 1972, and the following year Boris Bittker, a Yale law professor, published *The Case for Black Reparations*, which offered the first book-length legal analysis of the idea.[2] Bittker concluded that the exploitation of unpaid labor produced enormous economic benefits for the United States and that contemporary black Americans deserved to be compensated for past wrongs through some combination of lump-sum cash payments and preferential treatment in education and hiring.

Nevertheless, most prominent black civil rights leaders in the 1960s and '70s rejected the notion that blacks were owed a debt stemming from the country's slave past. An NAACP official dismissed reparations as "an illogical, diversionary and paltry way out for guilt-ridden whites."[3] Bayard Rustin, a Martin Luther King Jr. confidant and chief organizer of the 1963 March on Washington, also was skeptical of black efforts to cash in on the suffering of their ancestors. He called reparations demands "preposterous" and accused advocates of "hustling" and "begging." The "idea of reparations is a ridiculous idea," he said. "If my great-grandfather picked cotton for 50 years, then he may deserve some money, but he's dead and gone and nobody owes me anything."[4]

Renewed interested in slavery reparations came some two decades later, after Congress passed legislation in 1988 to provide payments to Japanese Americans who were sent to internment camps during World War II. The following year, John Conyers, a Democratic congressman from Michigan, introduced a bill to establish a federal task force to study reparations. Some form of that legislation has been introduced repeatedly ever since, but Congress has declined to approve the measure. Meanwhile, proponents have cited not only the Japanese American precedent but also Austria and Germany's payments to Holocaust survivors and Canada's compensation of indigenous former students who were separated from their families and forced to attend boarding schools.[5]

Conyers said reparations were warranted due to the "long-term residual impact of institutional racism that has persisted among African descendants through Jim Crow segregation, hate crime terrors of lynching and cross burning, and the disparate practices and policies of the prison industry, which in many ways has begun to re-enslave [blacks], who are disproportionately incarcerated and performing slave labor under the oppressive structure of disparate sentences." Black people, he continued, are "13 percent of America's population but account for more than 52 percent" of prison inmates, "notwithstanding the reality that Blacks are no more predisposed toward criminal behavior than any other population."[6]

Randall Robinson became the face of the reparations cause following the publication of his 2000 book, *The Debt: What America Owes Blacks*, which expands on Conyers's thesis regarding the downstream effects of slavery and segregation. "No race, no ethnic or religious group, has suffered so much over so long a span as blacks have, and still do, with the connivance of the United States government, from slavery and the century of legalized racial hostility that followed it," he wrote. "This book is about the great still-unfolding massive crime of official and unofficial America against Africa, African slaves, and their descendants in America."[7] Robinson was already a well-regarded international human rights activist best known for pressuring the US to confront the apartheid regime in South Africa. *The Debt* became a bestseller and helped to mainstream reparations advocacy. By the early 2000s it could plausibly be stated, as Robinson told the *New York Times*, that "there is no major black organization that does not support reparations."[8]

Still, the American public remained largely unpersuaded. In a 1997 ABC News poll, just 19 percent of respondents said the government should pay reparations.[9] The NAACP announced in 2005 that it would support efforts to take legal action against corporations with any history of involvement with slavery on the presumption that many of the problems blacks face today, "including poverty, disparities in health-care, and incarcerations can be directly tied to slavery."[10] But public support for this approach has likewise been tepid. A 2002 survey found that just one in five respondents thought "corporations should make cash payments to slaves' descendants. Among whites, support for cash payments was 6%, while among non-whites, 42% supported payments."[11]

Reparations lawsuits, meanwhile, have gone nowhere, mainly because slavery, however atrocious, was not illegal when it was practiced in the US, and the statute of limitations has long expired on claims being made by descendants of slaves. "Suing the government for condoning slavery will be impossible unless the government surrenders its sovereign immunity from civil suits," wrote Civil War historian Allen Guelzo. "Besides, the federal government never adopted a national slave code, and left slave legislation to the states." Nor is there a straightforward case for suing states. "In addition to the slave states of the old Confederacy, many Northern states also permitted slavery, but then abolished it voluntarily before 1820. Should Pennsylvania as well as Georgia be sued for reparations?"[12]

An appellate court dismissed a lawsuit in 1995 seeking more than $100 million from the federal government. "The

9th U.S. Circuit Court of Appeals, in its 3-0 ruling, reached the same conclusion as scores of lower-court judges who have considered similar reparations claims," a news outlet reported at the time.[13] A decade later, a suit brought against banks and insurance companies alleging that they had profited from slavery met a similar fate. An appellate court ruled that the plaintiffs lacked standing to sue on behalf of enslaved ancestors, concluding that the "causal chain is too long and has too many weak links for a court to be able to find that the defendants' conduct harmed the plaintiffs at all, let alone in an amount that could be estimated without the wildest speculation."[14]

Black support for reparations has consistently been higher than white support, but even among blacks it has varied significantly over the decades with no consistent pattern. According to Gallup, it climbed from 55 percent in 2002 to 73 percent in 2019. Over the same period, support rose from 6 to 16 percent for whites, and from 14 to 29 percent for all groups.[15] Yet a 2015 Kaiser Family Foundation/CNN poll found that 52 percent of blacks and 8 percent of whites agreed that the government should make cash payments to black Americans who are descendants of slaves.[16] The nation's appetite for reparations may reflect to some extent the state of race relations during a given period. The death in 2012 of Trayvon Martin, a black teenager shot by a neighborhood watchman, was followed by a series of high-profile incidents involving black suspects and police. These episodes culminated in the 2020 killing of George Floyd, which triggered nationwide protests that sometimes turned violent. Several of these encounters were captured by phone cameras and spread widely through social media, giving the public the impression that such incidents were commonplace.[17] In fact, police shootings had been declining for more than a half-century, and there was no evidence that cops were targeting blacks with lethal force.[18] Some argue that race relations soured after the election of Donald Trump in 2016, but data show that the phenomenon predates the first Trump presidency. A Gallup survey in 2015 found that 62 percent of respondents were dissatisfied with the state of race relations, up from 40 percent in 2008, which was the highest percentage since the early 1990s.[19] According to a CNN poll taken in October 2016, the month before Trump was elected, 54 percent of respondents said that relations between blacks and whites had worsened since Obama became president.[20]

Despite general black support for reparations in recent decades, the issue has continued to garner pointed criticism from prominent blacks on the political left and right who say reparations are unnecessary and potentially harmful to black self-development. "Reparations send a message to Americans of every other race that blacks are wards of the state because they are a broken people," wrote liberal journalist and author Juan Williams. "Social ills in the black community would be exaggerated as black people, flush with one big check, decide they don't need school, don't need a job, and remove themselves from the vitality of mainstream American life. Black people would be more highly stigmatized and stereotyped than ever before."[21] According to the conservative race scholar Shelby Steele, "when you trade on the past victimization of your own people, you trade honor for dollars. And this trading is only uglier when you are a mere descendant of those who suffered but nevertheless prevailed."[22]

Gregory Kane, a black newspaper columnist and commentator, faulted reparationists for failing "to acknowledge the significant role Africans played in the trans-Atlantic slave trade." As historians such as Ronald Segal and Hugh Thomas have documented, Kane noted in an academic paper, it was "primarily the Africans who waged war on and kidnapped their brethren and sold them to Europeans and Arabs." He continued:

> The wealth of evidence refuting the puerile assertion of "minimal" African involvement in trade is so compelling it is hard to know where to begin. Arabs enslaved Africans, subjecting them to the harsh plantation slavery that existed in the Western Hemisphere. While the institution of slavery in Arab and African societies did guarantee slaves more rights and freedoms than they had in the West, the process of enslavement itself was just as murderous and genocidal as the trip of Africans across the Middle passage.[23]

Brent Staples, a black editorial writer for the *New York Times*, allowed that "[t]argeted compensation is legal and just," but "the sweeping notion that individual black Americans are owed a 'debt' for slavery is a bridge too far. Black families have made and lost fortunes just as white families have. There is in addition no provable connection between 19th-century bondage and specific cases of 21st-century destitution."[24] Walter Williams, a black libertarian economist, called the whole debate a distraction. "The problems that black people face are not going to be solved by white people, and they're not going to be solved by money," he said. "The resources that are going into the fight for reparations would be far more valuably spent making sure that black kids have a credible education."[25] Another black economist, Glenn Loury, worried that reparations ultimately would undermine efforts to address racial inequality by allowing "the majority of Americans to look at the situation as one where 'we' do something for 'them'—alleviate their suffering, solve their problems, quiet their protests, and then, once the debt is paid off, wash our hands of society's inequities. Instead, we—meaning all Americans—should right racial inequities for the sake of the country."[26]

In his memoir, the tennis champion and civil rights activist Arthur Ashe wrote that calls for reparations, however warranted, promoted a counterproductive victimization mindset among blacks that ought to be discouraged rather than indulged. "I can understand the argument that blacks should have been paid reparations for slavery and segregation," he wrote. "We may indeed be entitled to something. But our sense of entitlement has been taken too far." Ashe, who was born in 1943 in the Jim Crow South and learned to play tennis on a segregated public playground in Richmond, Virginia, was especially concerned about the message that reparations activists were communicating to black youth. "One of the major tasks of my teachers as I grew up was to make sure that no black kid gave up the struggle to do better because of despair in the face of segregation. We were taught that segregation counted for nothing against our duty to ourselves to work hard and do well," he wrote. "Should we now give up because of an oppressive sense that we have not been compensated for historic wrongs done to us? Absolutely not."[27] Ashe articulated the ambivalence of many blacks when he put the reparations debate in the larger context of preferential policies:

> If American society had the strength to do what should be done to ensure that justice prevails for all, then affirmative action would be exposed for what it is: an insult to the people it is intended to help. What I and others want is an equal chance, under one set of rules, as on a tennis court.... Practically, affirmative action is probably necessary. But I would not want to know that I received a job simply because I am black. Affirmative action tends to undermine the spirit of individual initiative. Such is human nature; why struggle to succeed when you can have something for nothing?[28]

Other supporters of affirmative action who reject reparations include the Marxist political scientist Adolph Reed, who called the notion half-baked. "I've had this argument with the proponents of reparations. And my question for them all along has been, how can you imagine putting together a political alliance that would be broad enough so that you win on this issue," he said. "And if you can't imagine it, then what are you really doing? And their answer is, 'Well, don't you think black people deserve something?'" Reed's reply: "Well, a lot of people deserve a lot."[29]

Asked about reparations in 2007 on an NAACP presidential questionnaire, Barack Obama likewise expressed skepticism:

> I fear that reparations would be an excuse for some to say "we paid our debt" and to avoid the much harder work of enforcing our anti-discrimination laws in employment and housing; the much harder work of making sure that our schools are not separate and unequal; the much harder work of providing job training programs and rehabilitating young men coming out of prison every year; and the much harder work of lifting 37 million Americans of all races out of poverty. These challenges will not go away with reparations.[30]

Obama's resistance to reparations disappointed many black progressives, perhaps none more so than Ta-Nehisi Coates, whose widely discussed 2014 *Atlantic* magazine essay, "The Case for Reparations," probably did more to elevate the debate than any piece of writing since Randall Robinson's

The Debt. Still, Obama remained unconvinced. In a 2016 interview, he told Coates that "you can make a theoretical" argument in favor of compensating descendants of slaves, but other ways of helping the black underclass are more practical and less divisive. "Why are we even having the abstract conversation when we've got a big fight on our hands just to get strong, universal antipoverty programs and social programs in place, and we're still fighting to make sure that basic anti-discrimination laws are enforced," Obama said. "And those are fights that we can win because—and this is where I do believe America has changed—the majority, not by any means 100 percent, but the majority of Americans believe in the idea of nondiscrimination. They believe in the idea that Jamal and Johnny should be treated equally." Coates agreed with the president that racial attitudes had improved over the decades. But he insisted that America nevertheless had an obligation to take "responsibility for our history" and that monetary restitution for slavery and the decades of segregation that followed it was a proper means to that end.[31]

Coates's "case" for reparations amounts to a series of dubious moral, economic, and causal arguments that deserve far more scrutiny than they have received in the mainstream media or from scholars who presumably know better. The 1619 Project, a series of articles published by the *New York Times* in 2019 under the direction of Nikole Hannah-Jones, advances similarly questionable claims.* She and Coates

---

* The 1619 Project's title is a reference to the year African slaves first arrived in colonial Virginia.

share the same objective. "My ultimate goal is that there will be a reparations bill passed," Hannah-Jones told interviewers. "If you read the whole project, I don't think you can come away from it without understanding the project is an argument for reparations. You can't read it and not understand that something is owed."[32]

Coates, Hannah-Jones, and the 1619 Project attempt to "reframe" American history in a way that makes slave labor both its most salient characteristic and the main source of the country's future prosperity. "America begins in black plunder," according to Coates. "Nearly one-fourth of all white Southerners owned slaves, and upon their backs the economic basis of America—and much of the Atlantic world—was erected."[33] According to the *Times*'s Jake Silverstein, an editor of the 1619 Project, "Out of slavery—and the anti-black racism it required—grew nearly everything that has truly made America exceptional." Silverstein's examples in the service of this spectacular claim included the country's "economic might" and "industrial power," as well as its income inequality and health and education disparities. All of it, he asserted, stemmed from the enslavement of black people.[34] In her introductory essay, Hannah-Jones argued that the American War of Independence is best understood as a counterrevolution launched by the colonists, not to rebel against British rule but rather to defend slavery against looming British emancipation. "Conveniently left out of our founding mythology is the fact that one of the primary reasons the colonists decided to declare their independence from Britain was because they wanted to protect the institution of slavery," she wrote, "and some might argue that this nation was founded not as a democracy but as a slavocracy."[35] Hannah-Jones undoubtedly is correct that "some" might make such an argument, but leading scholars of the Colonial period, slavery, the American Revolution, and the Civil War are not among them. Like Coates, Hannah-Jones insists that the US has failed to take adequate responsibility for its slave past, and that the only way to rectify this is through racial preferences that include monetary reparations. "Race-neutral policies simply will not address the depth of disadvantage faced by people this country once believed were chattel," she asserted in a 2020 essay titled "What Is Owed." She continued, "Financial restitution cannot end racism, of course, but it can certainly mitigate racism's most devastating effects."[36] Really? In what way? And where are her examples of this happening?

While not a new phenomenon, it has become increasingly fashionable among public intellectuals to allow racial indignation to substitute for facts and logic. "I didn't know about the 1619 Project until it came out, and frankly when I learned about it my reaction was a big sigh," said Adolph Reed. "But again, the relation to history has passed to the appropriation of the past in support of whatever kind of 'justice' stories about the present are desired. This approach has taken root within the Academy. It's like all bets are off."[37] Progressive black writers such as Coates and Hannah-Jones have been able to capitalize on the trend Reed described because challenging their ideas in any serious way is politically incorrect. "On the issue of the Revolutionary War, Hannah-Jones's claim is quite simply false, but our current etiquette requires pretending that isn't true—because she's black," wrote John McWhorter of Columbia University. "Someone has received a Pulitzer Prize for a mistaken interpretation of historical documents about which legions of actual scholars are expert."[38] Black critics such as Reed and McWhorter who point out these distortions, false claims, key omissions, and factual errors are ignored or dismissed as Uncle Toms, while non-blacks who do so are accused of racism. Meanwhile, too many academics and media elites not only indulge this pseudo-scholarship but are eager to celebrate it. A 2017 profile of Coates in the *Chronicle of Higher Education* opened with the following:

> In March, some of the country's foremost historians gathered at the Radcliffe Institute for Advanced Study at Harvard University for a conference on "Universities and Slavery: Bound by History." Annette Gordon-Reed, Sven Beckert (who helped organize the conference), Craig Steven Wilder, and Adam Rothman were among the experts from more than 30 schools. More than 500 people attended, and the conference—which examined the delicate topic of Harvard's profits from slavery—was covered in *The New York Times*.
>
> And yet, for all the academic firepower in the room, the keynote speaker was someone who

lacks a university degree of any sort and has no scholarly publications to his name. But such is Ta-Nehisi Coates's standing in academe that he not only delivered the keynote but also sat down for a one-on-one session with Harvard's president, Drew Gilpin Faust. It is impossible to imagine any other journalist today being accorded the same privilege by professional historians.[39]

The attempt to make slavery pivotal to America's founding echoes the black nationalism of an earlier era, as does the attempt to silence dissent by playing the race card. The goal is greater power rather than greater knowledge or understanding. As Hannah-Jones wrote on social media, the 1619 Project is "about who gets control of the national narrative, and, therefore, the nation's shared memory of itself."[40] In another social media post, she dismissed her critics as "old white male historians."[41]

This has happened before. Other prominent scholars, including political liberals sympathetic to the efforts of black radicals in the 1960s, endured the same grilling. "Kenneth Stampp was told by militants that, as a white man, he had no right to write *The Peculiar Institution*," wrote University of Chicago historian Peter Novick. "Herbert Gutman, presenting a paper to the Association for the Study of Negro Life and History, was shouted down. A white colleague who was present (and had the same experience), reported that Gutman was 'shattered.' Gutman pleaded to no avail that he was 'extremely supportive of the black liberation movement—if people would just forget that I am white and hear what I'm saying.'"[42]

The 1619 Project deliberately limited the number of contributions from non-blacks and simply omitted essays from any scholars whose research challenged Hannah-Jones's distortions of American history. As the *Times* explained in a note to readers, "Almost every contributor in the magazine and special section—writers, photographers and artists—is black, a nonnegotiable aspect of the project that helps underscore its thesis."[43] Technically, the paper invited academic scholars to advise on the initiative, but according to the people who were consulted, their input was often rejected. Northwestern University historian Leslie Harris wrote that she "vigorously disputed" Hannah-Jones's claim about why the Revolutionary War was waged. "Slavery in the Colonies faced no immediate threat from Great Britain, so colonists wouldn't have needed to secede to protect it," Harris explained. "Despite my advice, the *Times* published the incorrect statement about the American Revolution anyway, in Hannah-Jones' introductory essay." Nor was this the only error that Harris pointed out to the *Times*. "In addition, the paper's characterizations of slavery in early America reflected laws and practices more common in the antebellum era than in Colonial times, and did not accurately illustrate the varied experiences of the first generation of enslaved people that arrived in Virginia in 1619."[44] Professor Gordon Wood of Brown University, who is perhaps the nation's leading authority on the American Revolution, wrote an open letter to the *New York Times* that took issue with the central thesis of the 1619 Project:

There is no evidence in 1776 of a rising movement to abolish the Atlantic slave trade, as the 1619 Project erroneously asserts, nor is there any evidence the British government was eager to do so. But even if either were the case, ending the Atlantic slave trade would have been welcomed by the Virginia planters, who already had more slaves than they needed. Indeed, the Virginians in the years following independence took the lead in moving to abolish the despicable international slave trade.

How could slavery be worth preserving for someone like John Adams, who hated slavery and owned no slaves? If anyone in the Continental Congress was responsible for the Declaration of Independence, it was Adams.... Ignoring his and other northerners' roles in the decision for independence can only undermine the credibility of your project with the general public. Far from preserving slavery, the North saw the Revolution as an opportunity to abolish the institution. The first anti-slave movements in the history of the world, supported by whites as well as blacks, took place in the northern states in the years immediately following 1776.[45]

The false history promoted by Ta-Nehisi Coates and Nikole Hannah-Jones has been adapted for a television series produced by Oprah Winfrey, and it's being taught in thousands of elementary and high schools nationwide.[46] As of 2020, more than 3,500 classrooms in all fifty states already were using a curriculum that grew out of the 1619 Project. In some school systems, including those in Chicago and Washington, DC, it had been adopted district-wide.[47] "Thousands of high schoolers are set to learn a radical new 'reparations math' curriculum that teaches how slavery 'led to a wealth gap for African Americans,'" the *Daily Mail* reported in 2023. "The course is the latest school module released by the 1619 Project's education network."[48] The upshot is that young, impressionable minds are being indoctrinated with political propaganda masquerading as scholarship, even as the central narratives of "The Case for Reparations" and the 1619 Project are rejected out of hand by the highest authorities on the subject matter.

The point is not that newspapers and periodicals should avoid these topics and instead leave them to the "experts." When professional journalists do weigh in, however, it is not too much to ask that they know what they're talking about and that they proceed in good faith. It is not too much to ask that they engage with the most respected research, deal in facts rather than speculation, and test competing claims against the evidence. The social justice advocates for reparations want to be exempted from such basic requirements out of a belief that they are operating on a higher moral plane than others. Yet the moral case for reparations ultimately rests on the notion that American slavery was uniquely evil, and that guilt is a heritable trait—like height or skin color—that can be passed

down from one generation to the next. Reparations proponents have failed to make a convincing case on either score.
"The wrongs of history have been invoked by many groups in
many countries as a moral claim for contemporary compensation," wrote Thomas Sowell, who has studied preferential
policies in the US as well as internationally. Yet "to transfer
benefits between two groups of living contemporaries because
of what happened between two sets of dead people is to raise
the question whether any sufferer is in fact being compensated. Only where both wrongs and compensation are viewed
as collectivized and inheritable does redressing the wrongs of
history have a moral, or even a logical, basis."[49]

Obviously, slavery wasn't unique to America. Slaves who
were brought here had been enslaved elsewhere by other
people before they arrived. Nor, in the main, were the slaves
who came to the Americas stolen by European slave traders.
When the Europeans arrived, most of Africa was run by Africans who had already been trafficking in slavery with Arabs
for centuries and who simply sold some of their own slaves to
these white men. Europeans didn't determine the rules and
conditions for trading African slaves. It was African rulers
who called the shots. "The overwhelming majority of slaves
were certainly obtained by the European traders in Africa by
purchase or negotiation with local rulers, merchants, or no-
bleman," wrote historian Hugh Thomas in his comprehensive
study of the Atlantic slave trade, while "only a small number
were obtained by Europeans by kidnapping." Jake Silverstein
and his colleagues at the *New York Times* might insist that

racism led to slavery, but the historical record clearly shows that racism was a consequence of slavery rather than a cause. "I think the 1619 Project very much promotes this, that slavery was created as a form of racial oppression, rather than a form of labor exploitation that ultimately became rationalized ideologically by racism," said the historian Thomas Mackaman.[50] Or as Sowell has written, "To make racism the driving force behind slavery is to make a historically recent factor the cause of an institution which originated thousands of years earlier."[51] Yes, theories about race and genetics were invoked in the US to defend slavery. If the Declaration of Independence said all men were equal, then slaves had to be considered less than human to justify the institution. But centuries before Europeans brought enslaved Africans to the Western Hemisphere, Europeans enslaved one another, just as Africans enslaved one another and Asians enslaved one another.[52] As Hugh Thomas explained, prior to the Atlantic slave trade and throughout history, it was more common for the slave and slaveholder to be of the same race:

> The Africans from whom the Europeans obtained most of the slaves to be shipped acquired them much as in antiquity in the Mediterranean, or in medieval Europe: first, as a result of war; second, in consequence of enslavement as a punishment for the people concerned; third, from poverty, resulting in someone's being constrained to sell his children, or even himself; or, fourth, from kidnapping,

which was as frequent among Africans as it was rare among Europeans.[53]

The trans-Atlantic slave trade gets far more attention from reparations advocates, but the trans-Saharan slave trade—which was operated by Arabs and transported captives from black Africa across the Sahara Desert and the Persian Gulf to the Islamic world of North Africa and the Middle East—involved a larger number of African slaves and lasted for a much longer period. "It is striking," wrote Harvard scholar Orlando Patterson, that "the total volume of African slaves acquired by Muslim masters is greater than the total acquired by Europeans in the Americas."[54] Nor could these Europeans have introduced human bondage to the Western Hemisphere, as the reparationists suggest, because it was already here before the first Europeans arrived. Slavery "was nothing new to the New World," anthropologist Peter Wood has noted. "It was an institution familiar to many native societies in both North and South America." Native Americans "had been enslaving one another, as far as we can tell, from time immemorial, and forced labor was far from the worst of it," he wrote. "Captured people fed the almost industrial level of human sacrifice at the center of the Aztec Empire. Some New World peoples captured and kept their enemies for rituals and the sport of torture and, in the case of cannibalistic societies, to maintain a mobile food supply."[55] Reparations advocates express outrage at slavery, but it's a highly selective, ideologically driven outrage based on a deliberately ahistorical reading of the past, one that tries to "erase Africa from the African slave trade," as historian James Oakes put it.[56]

"There is nothing notably peculiar about the institution of slavery," Patterson wrote in the opening pages of his definitive comparative study. "It has existed from before the dawn of human history right down to the twentieth century, in the most primitive of human societies and in the most civilized. There is no region of the earth that has not at some time harbored the institution. Probably there is no group of people whose ancestors were not at one time slaves or slaveholders."[57] Hugh Thomas documented not only that Africans enslaved Europeans but also that African slave masters treated European slaves no less inhumanely than Europeans treated African slaves. In the seventeenth century, Africans captured, utilized, and sold slaves from, among other places, Spain, France, Portugal, and Italy. "These slaves were treated with at least as much brutality as the African slaves were by Europeans," according to Thomas. Citing the contemporary account of William Atkins, an Englishman enslaved in Morocco in 1622, Thomas wrote: "Atkins described how a Frenchman, 'catched in the creeks of the river, with hopes to have escaped over in the night time,' was 'found by his patron, [who] first cut off his ears, then slit his nose, after that beat him with ropes till all his body which was not covered with gore was black with stripes, and lastly drove him naked, thus disfigured through the streets, for an example and a warning to other slaves not to try and escape.'"[58]

Hugh Thomas and Orlando Patterson are two highly respected scholars, and their findings are readily available to anyone writing about the history of slavery. Excluding their research in this area is not an oversight: It's an effort to push a certain narrative regardless of the facts. Writing about slavery in exclusively black-white terms, neglecting the non-Western societies where it flourished, and insisting that the institution was based on anti-black racism is intellectually dishonest. Ta-Nehisi Coates wants you to know that American slaves were "plundered of their bodies, plundered of their families, and plundered of their labor" to advance his moral case for reparations. He doesn't want to tell you about the African leaders who plundered their fellow black Africans before they arrived in the New World, or about the plundering of European bodies that occurred under the direction of Arabs who operated a trans-Saharan slave trade that lasted nearly thirteen centuries, or more than three times as long as the Atlantic slave trade.

Nikole Hannah-Jones wants you to know it is "not incidental that 10 of this nation's first 12 presidents were enslavers," and she insists that "neither [Thomas] Jefferson nor most of the founders intended to abolish slavery." But Jefferson's first draft of the Declaration of Independence, which criticized King George III for blocking colonial Virginia's attempts to ban slavery, doesn't jibe with that claim. Nor does this account of some of Jefferson's other anti-slavery efforts:

When Jefferson drafted a state constitution for Virginia in 1776, his draft included a clause prohibiting any more importation of slaves and, in 1783, Jefferson included in a new draft of a Virginia constitution a proposal for gradual emancipation of slaves. He was defeated in both these efforts. On the national scene, Jefferson returned to the battle once again in 1784, proposing a law declaring slavery illegal in all western territories of the country as it existed at that time. Such a ban would have kept slavery out of Alabama and Mississippi. The bill lost by one vote.... Afterwards, Jefferson said that the fate "of millions unborn" was "hanging on the tongue of one man, and heaven was silent in the awful moment."[59]

None of this excuses or negates the fact that Jefferson and other founders were slaveholders. But their views of the institution clearly were more complicated than the 1619 Project suggests. In the eighteenth and nineteenth century, proponents of emancipation were operating under constraints that Hannah-Jones has ignored out of ignorance or expedience. And her treatment of Abraham Lincoln is as careless as her treatment of Jefferson and the America Revolution. "Like many white Americans, he opposed slavery as a cruel system at odds with American ideals, but he also opposed black equality," she wrote of Lincoln. "He believed that free black people were a 'troublesome presence' incompatible with a democracy intended only for white people."[60] Two Princeton University historians, Allen Guelzo and Sean Wilentz, took Hannah-Jones to task for this shallow and dismissive characterization of Lincoln's views on slavery and blacks. "No president before Lincoln ever dared hint at putting an end to American slavery," Guelzo noted. "Lincoln, however, had never made any secret of his anti-slavery convictions. 'I am naturally anti-slavery,' he said. 'If slavery is not wrong, nothing is wrong. I cannot remember when I did not so think, and feel.'"[61]

Wilentz's numerous publications include *The Rise of American Democracy: Jefferson to Lincoln*, a book that won the 2006 Bancroft Prize, the highest honor for a historian. In a 2020 essay for the *Atlantic* magazine, Wilentz wrote that not only was Hannah-Jones's analysis of the American Revolution based on "false assertions" but also that her take on Lincoln was "built on partial truths and misstatement of the facts, which combine to impart a fundamentally misleading impression." Hannah-Jones "elides the crucial difference between Lincoln and the white supremacists who opposed him," wrote Wilentz.

> Lincoln asserted on many occasions, most notably during his famous debates with the racist Stephen A. Douglas in 1858, that the Declaration of Independence's famous precept that "all men are created equal" was a human universal that applied to black people as well as white people. Like the majority of white Americans of his time, including many radical abolitionists, Lincoln harbored the belief that white people were socially superior to black people. He insisted, however, that "in the right to eat

the bread without the leave of anybody else, which his own hand earns, [the Negro] is my equal, and the equal of Judge Douglas, and the equal of every other man." To state flatly, as Hannah-Jones's essay does, that Lincoln "opposed black equality" is to deny the very basis of his opposition to slavery.[62]

Hannah-Jones and the *New York Times* don't simply get basic facts wrong but get them wrong in ways that invalidate a central tenet of the 1619 Project, which is that racial discrimination and slavery formed the foundation of American history, and that slavery's long shadow continues to manifest itself to this very day. When James McPherson, the Civil War scholar and former president of the American Historical Association, was asked for his reaction to the 1619 Project, he said that he was "disturbed by what seemed like a very unbalanced, one-sided account, which lacked context and perspective on the complexity of slavery." In the United States, he added, "there was not only slavery but also an antislavery movement. So I thought the account, which emphasized America racism—which is obviously a major part of the history, no question about it—but it focused so narrowly on that part of the story that it left most of the history out."[63]

In other words, Hannah-Jones and the *New York Times* have falsified history to advance an ideological agenda. For example, Hannah-Jones wrote in her lead essay that in the struggle against slavery and racial animosity, "[f]or the most part, black Americans fought alone."[64] Asked about that remark, McPherson provides what Hannah-Jones leaves out. "From the Quakers in the eighteenth century, on through the abolitionists in the antebellum, to the radical Republicans in the Civil War and Reconstruction, to the NAACP which was an interracial organization founded in 1909, down through the civil rights movement in the 1950s and 1960s, there have been a lot of whites who have fought against slavery and racial discrimination, and against racism," he explained. "Almost from the beginning of American history that's been true. And that's what's missing from this perspective."[65]

These and other facts severely undermine the 1619 Project and, by extension, the moral case for slavery reparations that Ta-Nehisi Coates and others have presented. They illustrate both the illogic and impracticality of paying restitution to some people alive today based on what happened centuries ago to other people. Who, specifically, should pay reparations and who should receive them? And on what grounds, given that there's so much historical blame to spread around? Forced master-slave unions and the voluntary mixing of the races further complicates determining whether someone is a descendant of slaves, a descendant of slaveowners, or a descendant of both. Should black immigrants qualify? What about mixed-race individuals? Are descendants of Union soldiers killed in the Civil War exempt? Most white Americans trace their ancestry to people who came to the US after slavery ended and during the eras of mass immigration that began in the 1880s and 1960s. What do white descendants of people who were never slaveowners in America owe to black people who never suffered the cruelties of slavery, or to black West Indians and Nigerians who have migrated to the US and thus do not share the slave history of American blacks? By what logic are the grandchildren of Iranian refugees or Korean victims of Communism responsible for payouts to black Americans today, who happen to already be the wealthiest black people in the world?

As others have done, Coates cited as a precedent US payments to Japanese Americans and Germany's payments to Holocaust survivors. But in both cases, the claim was based on injury, not group identity. Money did not go to Japanese Americans as an ethnic group. It went only to those who were interned or to their immediate family members. Japanese Americans who were not interned received no money. "American law still operates under the Enlightenment assumption that rights belong to individuals, rather than to groups," wrote Allen Guelzo. "Reparations based on group identity run hard against the grain of treating Americans as individuals before the law."[66] Coates, Hannah-Jones, and others call for blacks *as a group* to receive slavery reparations, even though during the era of slavery there were thousands of free blacks, as well as thousands of black commercial slaveholders. While it's true that some blacks bought family members to emancipate them, there's also evidence, as historian Larry Koger and others have documented, that "[b]y and large, Negro slaveowners were darker copies of their white counterparts."[67] Reparationists do not sufficiently engage these counterarguments, express annoyance with people who raise them, and don't see the point in critics fussing over such details. For them, the tremendous cost of the Civil War in blood and treasure counts for nothing in weighing the "debt" that the nation supposedly owes black Americans. It counts for nothing, as journalist Karl Zinsmeister has noted, "that the majority of today's Americans descend from people who were not even in America when slavery was practiced. And of the people who were here, a much larger number fought against slavery than practiced it."[68]

For reparationists, this is nitpicking. "The problem of reparations has never been practicality," according to Coates. "It has always been the awesome ghosts of history."[69] But there's no need to drag the supernatural into this discussion. In the real world, the challenge is the pragmatism of granting reparations in the twenty-first century. America today is an ethnically diverse democracy where small majorities of a minority group (blacks) support reparations and large majorities of whites do not. It's also a country where preference policies for blacks have tended to expand to other groups, such as Hispanics, Asian Americans, and women. If blacks are deserving of compensation for past mistreatment, why not the descendants of Irish migrants who faced employment discrimination, women who were denied the franchise, Jews who faced anti-Semitism in the academy, or Asian migrants who were lynched, forced to attend segregated schools, and denied property rights?

The economic argument for reparations is perhaps even weaker than the moral case that proponents present, insofar as it rests on easily contestable presumptions that America's wealth resulted from the exploitation of black people, and that were it not for this exploitation, today's racial inequality would not exist. There is no question that some individual slaveholders became very wealthy, but reparations activists argue that slavery was how American society as a whole became more prosperous. If reparations are about sharing the net financial gains that came from exploiting black labor, it must first be established that slavery produced net financial gains for America. Economists and historians have debated the relationship between slave labor and capitalism for more than a century. The academic literature is vast, and the debate remains unsettled.[70]

Ta-Nehisi Coates made a direct connection between slavery, rising American wealth, and today's racial disparities in written testimony before Congress in 2019. "As historian Ed Baptist has written, enslavement 'shaped every crucial aspect of the economy and politics' of America, so that by 1836 more than $600 million, almost half of the economic activity in the United States, derived directly or indirectly from the cotton produced by the million-odd slaves," Coates said. "By the time the enslaved were emancipated, they comprised the largest single asset in America. Three billion in 1860 dollars, more than all the other assets in the country combined."[71]

Other scholars, however, have pointedly questioned Baptist's methodology. "Baptist's statistic is demonstrably wrong," wrote historian Wilfred McClay. It's "based on elementary accounting errors, incorrectly double- and triple-counting intermediate transaction costs in a way that greatly inflates the final figure. The correct number should have been closer to 5 percent than 50."[72] Similarly, in his 1619 Project essay, the sociologist Matthew Desmond argued that slavery "was undeniably a font of phenomenal wealth," that cotton "was the nation's most valuable export," and that when the Civil War began, "the Mississippi Valley was home to more millionaires per capita than anywhere else in United States."[73] Yet the economist Deirdre McCloskey maintains that "each step in the logic of the King Cotton historians is mistaken." The institution of slavery "made a few Southerners rich; a few Northerners, too. But it was ingenuity and innovation that enriched Americans generally, including at last the descendants of the slaves." More broadly, the "enrichment of the modern world did not depend on cotton textiles," according to McCloskey. "Cotton mills, true, were pioneers of some industrial techniques, techniques applied to wool and linen as well. And many other techniques, in iron making and engineering and mining and farming, had nothing to do with cotton. Britain in 1790 and the U.S. in 1860 were not nation-sized cotton mills." Both countries "would have become just as rich without the 250 years of unrequited toil. They have remained rich, observe, even after the peculiar institution was abolished, because their riches did not depend on its sinfulness."[74]

The reparationists are attempting to use the country's slave past to launch ideological attacks on free-market capitalism today, unbothered by the fact that it is under a capitalist system that American blacks have become by far the richest black people in the world. "Desmond projects slavery's legacy onto a litany of tropes about rising inequality, the decline of labor-union power, environmental destruction, and the 2008 financial crisis," explained Phillip Magness, an economic historian. "The intended message is clear: modern capitalism carries with it the stain of slavery, and its putative excesses are proof of its continued brutality. It follows that only by abandoning the free market and embracing political redistribution will we ever atone for this tainted inheritance."[75]

If a noisy debate continues over the role of plantation slavery in the industrial development of the United States, what's harder to dispute is that the Deep South, where slavery was concentrated, was the poorest region of the country before and after the Civil War, and that this was true for Southern whites and blacks alike. If slave labor enriches not just individual slaveholders but also a whole society, how is it that Brazil, which had a much larger slave population than the US, never became as wealthy as the US? Moreover, those areas of Brazil where slavery flourished were also the most impoverished areas of the country. Brazil was the last nation in the Western Hemisphere to abolish slavery, and when it did so it was still an economically underdeveloped country.[76] Likewise in the US, on the eve of the Civil War the Mississippi Valley may have been able to boast more millionaires per capita than any other region, but the South was still the country's poorest region, and "those parts of the South where slavery was concentrated—Mississippi and Alabama, for example—have long been among the poorest parts of the

South," one analysis observed. "In short, just as slavery permitted some whites to benefit at the expense of blacks…so it could permit the whole slave system to profit while imposing a loss on the larger southern society of which it was a part."[77]

In his account of free blacks in the antebellum South, Ira Berlin wrote that even though whites "valued the benefits they wrung from slave labor and showed little disposition to relinquish them," they also "commonly lamented the ill effects of bondage" on white Southerners generally. Slavery "devalued labor in the white man's eyes, deterred immigrants from settling in the South, drove off ambitious youth, and discouraged industry among those who remained," Berlin wrote. "Casting a jealous eye on the rapid growth of population and wealth in the North, many Upper South whites openly denounced slavery as a drag on the economic development of the region."[78] These are among the reasons why the South lagged the North economically during slavery and in its aftermath, notwithstanding the presence of wealthy individual slaveholders. Those who support reparations argue that all whites benefited from the enslavement of blacks, along with the country as a whole. Yet the evidence suggests that on balance slavery had a negative social and economic impact on all Americans, and especially on those in closest proximity to the institution. A separate study of the period put it this way:

> The larger southern society paid the price of slavery in many ways, one of which was the negative attitude toward economic activity in general and

work in particular which developed among its white population. The overwhelming majority of white southerners owned no slaves, so that their economic well-being depended upon their own efforts. The southern culture, bred by a slave-owning aristocracy, downgraded economic efficiency, economic motivation, and especially hard, steady work by a white man. Slave societies in general tend to make work somewhat dishonorable in the eyes of free men. Whatever the psychological mechanism or principle, it is empirically apparent from numerous contemporary accounts of the antebellum South that its white people worked less, less carefully, less steadily, and less effectively than those in the rest of the country.[79]

Advocates of preferential policies take it as a given that past discrimination is the main cause of today's statistical disparities. For a century after the Civil War, Coates argued, blacks were subjected to convict leasing, redlining, poll taxes, and sundry other humiliations. As he sees it, this is why the "typical black family in this country has one-tenth the wealth of the typical white family," why "black women die in childbirth at four times the rate of white women," and why the US has "the largest prison population on the planet, of which the descendants of the enslaved make up the largest share."[80] There are several problems with this argument, which is rooted in an assumption that disproportionate group outcomes in a multiethnic society are uncommon and necessarily the result of discrimination. Yet that assumption can't withstand some very basic scrutiny. According to the Pew Research Center, the wealth gap between Asians and Hispanics in 2021 was larger than the wealth gap between whites and blacks.[81] Clearly something other than racism, past or present, can be responsible for wealth differences, though Coates seems to believe that no other explanations are worth exploring. Moreover, Pew reported that the median Asian household was worth considerably more than the median white household, which likewise undermines the white supremacist explanation for racial disparities in group net worth.

Although it's true that maternity mortality rates are significantly higher among blacks than among other groups, it's also true that Hispanics and Asian Americans have had lower maternal mortality rates than whites.[82] Research also has shown that nonracial factors are likely driving the higher death rates among blacks. "Black women tend to become pregnant when they are younger than White women," and "tend to have more underlying 'comorbid' conditions such as obesity, diabetes, and hypertension," and "tend to not seek prenatal care as often as White women," wrote Stanley Goldfarb, a former associate dean at the University of Pennsylvania medical school. "Each of these factors is associated with increased complications of pregnancy unrelated to skin color."[83]

Complaints about racial imbalance in the prison population often leave out, as Coates did, any mention of the racial imbalance in criminal behavior generally, and acts of violent crime in particular. Blaming Jim Crow–era discrimination for high black incarceration rates today requires ignoring the fact that black violent crime rates during the Jim Crow era were significantly lower than they would become by the end of the twentieth century. "While young black men were murdered at the rate of about 45 per 100,000 in 1960, by 1990 the rate was 140 per 100,000," wrote legal scholar Randall Kennedy.[84] Was there more racism in 1990 than in 1960? The "high rates of black violence in the late twentieth century are a matter of historical fact, not bigoted imagination," according to another study. "The trends reached their peak not in the land of Jim Crow but in the more civilized North, and not in the age of segregation but in the decades that saw the rise of civil rights for African Americans—and of African American control of city government."[85] The antisocial behavior that leads to the arrest and incarceration of so many young men has more to do with fatherless homes than systemic racism. This, too, is a more recent phenomenon that progressives don't want to acknowledge. Black marriage rates surpassed white marriage rates in the first four decades of the twentieth century, and black nuclear families were much more common in 1920 than they were in 2020, which is one reason black communities were much safer notwithstanding the much higher levels of black poverty at the time. "Virtually every major social pathology," political scientist Stephen Baskerville noted, "has been linked to fatherless children: violent crime, drug and alcohol abuse, truancy, unwed pregnancy, suicide, and psychological disorders—all correlating more strongly with fatherlessness than with any other single factor, surpassing even race and poverty."[86]

The idea that but for slavery and segregation, we would see racially proportionate outcomes among black Americans in everything from labor force participation and earnings to academic achievement, homeownership, criminal behavior, and even health outcomes doesn't come close to passing scrutiny. By this reasoning, if blacks comprise 13 percent of a given population, it follows that they should comprise a roughly similar percentage of black judges, firefighters, high school principals, prison inmates, drivers ticketed for speeding, millionaires, and freshmen at the University of Michigan. Yet there is no historical or logical basis for presupposing a random or even distribution of peoples in various institutions, behaviors, pursuits, and accomplishments. Scholars who have studied societies down through history don't find the proportionate outcomes that proponents of preferential policies use as a baseline.

David Landes's acclaimed history of global inequality, *The Wealth and Poverty of Nations*, opens with a chapter titled "Nature's Inequalities," in which he states flatly that the "world has never been a level playing field."[87] Moreover, it has been commonplace for outcomes to differ not only between countries but among the population of a given country, especially a country comprised of people from different racial and ethnic backgrounds. "All multi-ethnic societies exhibit a tendency for ethnic groups to engage in different occupations, have different levels (and, often, types) of education, receive different incomes, and occupy a different place in the social hierarchy," wrote Myron Weiner, a political scientist at MIT who studied multiethnic societies around the world.[88] Another comparative analysis of ethnic groups internationally, by Donald Horowitz of Duke University, concluded that "few, if any, societies" had ever approximated a situation where "all groups are proportionately represented at all levels in all sectors of the economy."[89]

These findings work against the notion that disparate outcomes, either between countries or within countries, are anomalous or necessarily sinister as opposed to ordinary and naturally occurring. Coates's monocausal explanation for current racial gaps in the US is past discrimination, but as discussed in Chapter 1, there are significant social and economic disparities among whites that racial discrimination simply cannot explain. There are also multiple examples of racial and ethnic minorities groups in the US who outperform the white majority, and examples of black Americans outperforming other groups who have experienced less discrimination. None of this would be possible if in fact past discrimination alone was a satisfactory explanation for uneven outcomes.

According to recent census data, per capita median incomes of Americans of Chinese and Japanese ancestry were higher than those of white Americans, even though both ethnicities have faced significant past discrimination in the US, including lynchings, school segregation, restricted property rights, and forced internment.[90] Incomes of Indian Americans and Korean Americans also exceeded those of whites, according to the census.[91] Meanwhile, black per capita incomes were higher than Hispanic per capita incomes, even though it would be difficult to argue convincingly that Hispanics have been treated worse in the US than blacks have been treated.[92] A study of bullying in New York City public schools found that physical and verbal attacks on Chinese students far outnumbered those directed at blacks and Latinos, yet Chinese and other Asian Americans have long outperformed other groups, including whites, both in the classroom and the workplace. On average, Asians have higher grades, higher scores on standardized tests, and are more likely to acquire a degree from an elite university.[93] Those eager to attribute academic disparities to racial oppression may be overlooking a far more mundane explanation. A reliable predictor of school performance is study habits, and research shows that Asians spend more time than other groups hitting the books. One survey of twenty thousand students in nine schools in California and Wisconsin found that Asian American high school students spent twice as much time doing homework as non-Asians did.[94]

Those trying to "prove" that discrimination is the only plausible explanation for differences in black-white outcomes typically omit Asian outcomes from their analyses. That's because including Asians would significantly undermine their efforts to blame intergroup differences on racial bias. Two typical examples are racial disparities in bank loans and school suspensions, which we are told can be blamed, respectively, on racist lenders and educators. However, the same studies that show blacks having their conventional mortgage applications denied at a higher rate than whites also show whites being denied at a higher rate than Asian applicants.[95] Clearly, banks are not discriminating against whites and in favor of Asians, so obviously something other than racial bias—such as net wealth, credit history, outstanding debt, and so forth, all of which can vary from one group to another—must be driving the discrepancy in loan approvals. Similarly, studies showing that black students are more likely than white students to be disciplined in school also indicate that whites are disciplined at much higher rates than Asians, yet the latter fact often goes unmentioned, lest it undermine a preferred race-based narrative. Nevertheless, family structure is a stronger predictor than race when it comes to which students are suspended or expelled. It's no accident, one study concluded, "that the group with the lowest disciplinary index—Asians—also has the lowest proportion of students from single parent families. Indeed, one can predict a group's discipline index quite reliably simply by knowing the proportion of its children living with two parents."[96] In a 2019 report by the Institute for Family Studies, sociologists Nicholas Zill and W. Bradford Wilcox found that black students living with both married parents had suspension rates that not only were less than half as large as those for other blacks, but also less than the suspension rate for white students from families that weren't intact.[97] None of this means that there are no racist bankers or school personnel, but it does suggest that statistical disparities can't automatically be equated with discrimination.

A direct connection between discrimination and upward mobility is also complicated by the experience of black West Indians living in the US. Comparisons between immigrant and native populations are complicated by the fact that immigrants are self-selecting, meaning that they tend to be more able and ambitious than those who choose to remain in their homeland. One way to control for selectivity bias is to focus on second-generation immigrants who did not make the decision to migrate. Comparisons between native black Americans and the descendants of black West Indians can be instructive for the purposes of assessing the role of past and present racism in black outcomes because the two groups not only share physical features but also a legacy of plantation slavery and racial oppression.

In his study of second-generation West Indians in New York City, Van C. Tran of Columbia University found that they were as likely as native black Americans "to live in highly segregated neighborhoods, with similar structural constraints and physical environments," and just as likely to "experience discrimination and prejudice from native whites and others, because internal ethnic distinctions among blacks often elude many native whites." Nevertheless, on the most common measures of socioeconomic well-being, "Native blacks reported the most disadvantaged outcomes, while West Indians reported outcomes similar to those of native whites." Tran found that "11.4 percent of the native black sample did not have a high school education, compared to only 6.9 percent of West Indians and 4.2 percent of native whites." Black natives were "twice as likely to be unemployed compared to West Indians (11.8 percent) and native whites (9.1 percent)." Second-generation West Indians "are much less likely than native blacks to drop out of high school, be unemployed, be idle, or have a child by the age of 18," according to Tran. "They are also much more likely than native blacks to have graduated from college and to be in a professional occupation by the age of 25."[98] Other studies of second-generation Caribbean immigrants in New York City showed that employment rates "exceeded those of whites," that the young men had significantly lower arrest rates than their native black counterparts, and that Caribbean household incomes on average exceeded those of both black natives and white natives.[99]

Kamala Harris argued for reparations in 2019, when she told National Public Radio that slavery led to "generations of people experiencing the highest forms of trauma" down to this day.[100] But second-generation black West Indians are an example of a group that shares this traumatic past yet has outperformed both black natives and white natives. Aside from the counterexamples, there is also a problem with the principle that Harris and others have relied upon. Inherited trauma makes no more sense than inherited guilt, and no reasonable person would apply such a standard consistently across all groups. As the writer Coleman Hughes has noted, "If it were true that people inherited the trauma experienced by their distant ancestors, then not just black Americans but virtually all people would be traumatized. What human alive today doesn't have ancestors who suffered trauma?"[101]

Slavery's harm to slaves is not in dispute, but its harm to descendants of slaves more than 150 years after the end of the Civil War is speculative. The notion that racial disparities in the twenty-first century are directly linked to the slave era is based more on ideology than hard evidence. In fact, a strong argument could be made that US descendants of African slaves are better off because their ancestors were brought to America, even though the slaves themselves obviously were not better off. In the first one hundred years after slavery, blacks made tremendous social and economic gains, as this volume has documented. Black retrogression in areas such as crime, welfare dependency, and labor force participation date to the post-1960s era, suggesting that present-day racial inequality is mainly a function of factors other than the legacy of slavery and segregation.[102]

In more recent years, the nation's history of state-sanctioned "redlining," or denying people access to credit because of where they live, has emerged as one of the leading arguments for black redress. California, New York, and other states that organized commissions to study reparations after

the death of George Floyd in 2020 cited lending discrimination as a major justification. Because homeownership can
play such a central role in accumulating wealth, the fact that
blacks were denied home loans is said to be a root cause of
today's racial wealth gap.

The Federal Housing Administration (FHA) and the
Home Owners' Loan Corporation (HOLC) were agencies
established in the 1930s to facilitate homeownership. HOLC
purchased and refinanced troubled mortgages while FHA in-
sured mortgages and home-maintenance loans. Prior to the
1930s, people typically paid cash for homes or were required
to make down payments of at least 30 percent, an amount
few could afford. The new agencies were intended to make
mortgages more widely available, and the effort was remarkably successful. Between 1933 and 1941, housing starts grew
by 566 percent. After World War II, according to historian
Kenneth Jackson, "the number became even larger, and by
the end of 1972, FHA had helped nearly eleven million families to own houses and another twenty-two million families
to improve their properties."[103]

HOLC stopped lending in 1936, after having purchased
and refinanced more than one million mortgages. It then created a series of maps to manage its portfolio and assess credit
risk at the neighborhood level in more than two hundred cities. The highest-rated neighborhoods received an A grade and
were marked in green, while the lowest-rated neighborhoods
received a D grade and were marked in red. "The concentration of black households in the highest-risk zones on these

maps often has been noted by scholars and policymakers, and accordingly, these maps have become a visual shorthand for government-sponsored housing market discrimination in American cities," according to a 2021 National Bureau of Economic Research paper by economic historian Price V. Fishback and three coauthors. Yet, "the HOLC created its system of maps after the agency had finished making all of its loans. Consequently, the famous color-coded maps were not used to deny access to mortgage financing."[104] Some have speculated that FHA later relied on HOLC surveys to create their own redlining maps, but "to date, it has not been possible to systematically examine the similarity of the two sets of maps because the FHA redlining maps were apparently destroyed sometime around 1970."[105]

In any case, Fishback and his coauthors conclude, the evidence that survives suggests that FHA did not use the redlining maps to discriminate against blacks. "A comparison of black and white neighborhoods that were redlined by HOLC shows that, on average, redlined white neighborhoods had better census economic characteristics compared with redlined black neighborhoods, the opposite of what we'd expect to see if black neighborhoods had been targeted for the lowest security grade because of race."[106] That is, if FHA policy reflected racial bias against blacks, you'd expect to see black neighborhoods with better economic characteristics than whites nevertheless receive the lowest credit rating possible, a D. Instead, the data showed that white neighborhoods with better economic characteristics than black neighborhoods were awarded a D. The authors also found that while a higher percentage of the black population lived in redlined areas, most residents of neighborhoods where FHA refused to insure mortgages weren't black. "In our sample, over 95 percent of black homeowners lived in the lowest-rated 'D' zones. Yet, the vast majority (92 percent) of the total redlined home-owning population was white."[107] If being a victim of redlining is a qualification for reparations, what is the argument for excluding descendants of white redlined households?

Again, the point here is not to deny the fact that discrimination against blacks limited their housing options. The question is whether anti-black housing discrimination suffices as an explanation for today's wealth gap and thus warrants race-based monetary compensation. And the reality is that notwithstanding the difficulties that blacks faced in obtaining mortgages in the postwar period, homeownership among blacks rose faster than it did among whites. Research by economists William J. Collins and Robert A. Margo demonstrated that between 1940 and 1980, homeownership climbed by 37 percentage points for blacks and by 34 points for whites.[108]

The case for reparations ultimately amounts to a string of "what if" arguments. If blacks hadn't been enslaved and subject to Jim Crow, it is assumed, here is where they would be today in terms of educational attainment, income, health care, incarceration rates, homeownership, representation in skilled professions, and so forth. But all of this is ridiculous speculation by people claiming to know the ultimate source of intergroup differences. To claim that black Americans living today would be better off if their African ancestors had not been sold into slavery is to invite a comparison of outcomes between the descendants of black Africans who never came to the US and those who did. And it's abundantly clear that despite centuries of slavery and Jim Crow, black Americans today are far better off than black people who never left Africa.

FIVE

The Affirmative Action Era

A History of Retrogression

T he ability of racial preferences to stigmatize black achievements first hit home for me in college in the early 1990s.
Just before the start of my senior year, I received a job offer
from the local newspaper. A short time later, I happened to
run into a former editor of the college paper where I had previously worked and told her the news. "Congratulations,"
she said. "I heard they were looking for more minorities."
I was on friendly terms with this person, so I don't think it
was her intention was to offend, but the remark still stung.
For me, the episode illustrated one of the major downsides

of affirmative-action policies. No one with any self-respect wants to be perceived as a token, whether in the workplace or on a college campus, and racial preferences can facilitate those kinds of assumptions even for the most accomplished black professionals.

In his memoir, the black scholar Thomas Sowell described the change in how black success was perceived by others over the decades. "One of the ironies that I experienced in my own career was that I received more automatic respect when I first began teaching in 1962, as an inexperienced young man with no Ph.D. and few publications, than later on in the 1970s, after accumulating a more substantial record," he wrote. "What happened in between was 'affirmative action' hiring of minority faculty."[1]

To illustrate the point, Mr. Sowell recounted a student approaching him after class at UCLA, where he taught economics in the 1970s. The student was having trouble understanding something in the textbook, and Mr. Sowell explained to him what it meant. "Are you sure?" the student said.

"Yes, I'm sure," Sowell replied. "I wrote the textbook." The student then noticed the name on the cover and was "obviously embarrassed," Sowell wrote. "It was one of the signs of the times, one of the fruits of 'affirmative action.'"[2]

A similar personal story about white perceptions and black self-doubt is related by the black economist Walter Williams, who taught at Temple University in Philadelphia in the 1970s:

[M]y duties included teaching the PhD microeconomics seminar and serving on the PhD examination committee. Having a black student in my graduate class was rare. During the first few class meetings, some of the whites would ask searching questions that sometimes required that I go through a mathematical proof.

Although I never suggested this to students, it was my impression—not born of paranoia, I trust— that they were testing my credentials, checking to see whether I was competent in my subject. I'd simply answer their question and move on. After a few classes that kind of questioning stopped. In the rare cases when the class did include a black student, who might have sensed what was going on, I could almost read a sigh of relief on his face. Maybe he said to himself, with relief, "The brother could answer the question!"[3]

Sowell considered it "fortuitous" that his academic achievements predated racial preferences. "My academic career began two years before the Civil Rights Act of 1964 and I received tenure a year before federal 'goals and timetables' were mandated under affirmative action policies," he wrote. "[T]hese facts spared me the hang-ups afflicting many other black intellectuals, who were haunted by the idea that they owed their careers to affirmative action." Another way that timing worked to Sowell's benefit? "I happened to come along right after the worst of the old discrimination was no longer there to impede me and just before racial quotas made the achievements of blacks look suspect."[4]

Supreme Court Justice Clarence Thomas, who graduated from Yale Law School in 1974, recalled that he was treated "dismissively" at the time by job recruiters, who "asked pointed questions unsubtly suggesting that they doubted I was as smart as my grades indicated." Eventually, he stopped pursuing work in a big-city law firm and accepted a job in the state attorney general's office in Missouri. "Now I knew what a law degree from Yale was worth when it bore the taint of racial preference."[5] Thomas has been labeled a hypocrite for opposing racial preferences because he supposedly benefited from them as a college student, yet no one has produced evidence that race played a role in his admission to the College of the Holy Cross or Yale Law School.

According to press accounts, he was recruited to Holy Cross by a dean, John Brooks, who wanted to increase the number of black students on campus, but Thomas has long denied that story.[6] He started college at Immaculate Conception, a seminary in Missouri, but left after a year and returned home to Savannah, Georgia. In his memoir, he said that he applied to Holy Cross at the urging of a nun who had taught him in high school. "I ranked near the top of my class at Immaculate Conception, so Holy Cross had quickly accepted my application," he wrote. "The only problem was money, but the director of financial aid told me that something could be worked out."[7] It's true that some black students who had been contacted by Brooks were admitted to Holy Cross the same year that Thomas transferred there, but the justice has shot down the suggestion that he was one of Brooks's recruits. "A nun suggested Holy Cross. That's how I wound up there," he told a reporter in 2007. "Your industry"—the media—"has suggested that we were all recruited. That's a lie. Really, it's a lie. I don't mean a mistake. It's a lie." The "thing that has astounded me over the years is that there has been such an effort to roll that class into people's notion of affirmative action," he added. "You hear this junk. It's just not consistent with what really happened."[8]

Nor is there any evidence that Thomas, who turned down offers from Harvard Law School and the University of Pennsylvania Law School, was admitted to Yale Law School under its affirmative-action program rather than through the regular admissions process.[9] He had graduated from Holy Cross ninth in his class (of more than five hundred students).[10] According to the New York Times, eight Holy Cross graduates were admitted to Yale Law between 1968 and 1978, the decade that included Thomas's law school career.[11] Why assume that he got in only because of his race? Why question Thomas's credentials but not those of Bill Clinton or Hillary Rodham, two of his fellow Yale Law students? The reason is affirmative action, which has helped to delegitimize black academic and professional success.

Chief Justice John Roberts's majority opinion in Students for Fair Admissions v. Harvard stressed that race-conscious admissions violate the Equal Protection Clause of the Fourteenth Amendment. But that's not the only problem with them, and Thomas performed a public service in his concurrence by detailing the harm that racial favoritism inflicts not only on those from non-favored groups but also on the intended beneficiaries. When blacks and Hispanics "take positions in the highest places of government, industry or academia," Thomas wrote, "it is an open question... whether their skin color played a part in their advancement." He spoke from experience.

It is impossible to know for certain exactly where black Americans would be if not for a half-century of affirmative action, but there is a sizeable amount of evidence that these policies have on balance been more harmful than helpful. Blacks have progressed faster when the focus has been on equal treatment rather than special treatment, when intact black families were more common, when poor black neighborhoods had lower rates of violent crime, and when the welfare state was smaller. The desegregation of schools and institutions that began in the 1950s and continued in the '60s has been far more important to the creation and expansion of the black middle class than the racial preferences and anti-poverty programs of the 1970s and '80s. And the rate at which the black middle class grows has tended to coincide with the rate at which the overall economy was growing.

Census data show that between 1950 and 1970, the percentage of professionals and managers rose by 198 percent for black males and by 48 percent for white males. However, between 1970 and 1990—the first two decades of affirmative action— the increase was 27 percent for black males and 3 percent for white males. The story for female professionals and managers is similar. Between 1950 and 1970, the percentage grew by 90 percent for black women and by 9 percent for white women, but over the next two decades growth fell to 70 percent and 56 percent, respectively.[12] Clearly, black fortunes were improving faster for men and women in the decades prior to affirmative action. To credit racial preferences for this advancement is to willfully ignore previous trend lines. National economic trends at the time also can't be ignored. Economic growth averaged 4 percent in the 1950s and 4.1 percent in the 1960s, but that rate fell to 2.8 percent in the 1970s and to 2.7 percent in the 1980s. This means that growth in the 1980s was only about 65 percent of what it averaged in the 1960s.[13] Apparently, the combination of equal opportunities and faster economic growth are more important than preferential policies when it comes to increasing the number of black professionals.

More blacks in middle-class jobs should translate into higher black earnings, but here, too, the evidence shows that the affirmative action policies coincided with slower income growth, stagnation, and even retrogression. An analysis of racial differences in earnings over a seventy-year period found that "after narrowing consistently from 1940 to 1970, the black-white difference in median annual earnings among all men has since widened substantially, growing by the end of the Great Recession to its size in 1950."[14] Economist Robert

A. Margo of Boston University likewise noticed that between 1940 and 1960, the ratio at which blacks increased their earnings relative to whites "grows at a steady pace, which then accelerates in the 1960s. But in the late 1970s the upward trend loses steam, and the pace of convergence after 1980 was much slower than during the proceeding four decades."[15]

Citing federal data, the journalist Bob Zelnick reported that after accounting for inflation, the median income of black families in 1993 was not statistically different from their income in 1969. Among white families, median income grew by more than 9 percent over the same period. Overall, reductions in income inequality between black and white earners stalled under affirmative action. Black married couples, however, were an exception. "The ratio of black:white median family income was 0.61 percent in 1969 and had declined to 0.55 percent in 1993, reflecting in part the larger drop in black families maintained by married couples," Zelnick surmised. "By contrast, black families headed by married couples gained 31 percent in family income," which means they climbed "from 72 percent to 81 percent of the white level."[16] In the first half of the twentieth century, black labor force participation rates were higher or comparable to those of whites, and even though blacks were still living under Jim Crow laws, fatherless black households had yet to become the norm, as would be the case by the 1980s. The role of the black nuclear family has received far less attention than the role of racial preferences in black progress, but that's an example of ideology trumping logic, evidence, and real-world experience.

Racial preferences and a rapidly expanding welfare state seemed to have done little to address black poverty, as well. "In 1993, 31 percent of black families and 8 percent of white families were poor; in 1969, 28 percent of black families and 8 percent of white families were poor," Zelnick wrote.[17] Compare that track record with poverty reduction in the decades leading up to the era of affirmative action, when the percentage of black families living below the poverty line plummeted from 87 percent in 1940, to 47 percent in 1960, to 30 percent in 1970.[18] There's really no comparison.

A common criticism of race-preferences policies is that most of the benefits tend to go to those blacks who are already better off rather than to the black underclass, and hard data validates that view.[19] A larger black professional class is a welcome development, but don't forget that affirmative action was sold as a way to help the black poor escape poverty. Nevertheless, the plight of the black underclass worsened under race preferences, as evidenced by rising income inequality among the black population. "In 1968 four-fifths of poorly educated central-city black male residents held jobs; by 1992 fewer than half worked," wrote political scientist Jennifer L. Hochschild.[20] "Segregation by income among black families was lower than among white families in 1970, but grew four times as much between 1970 and 2007," according to a 2011 study by two Stanford University scholars. "By 2007, income segregation among black families was 60 percent greater than among white families."[21] Between 1967 and 1992, the share of total black income that went to the top 20 percent of black earners rose at a rate that was similar to their white counterparts. But over the same period, blacks in the lowest 20 percent of earners saw their share of total black income decline at more than twice the rate of comparably situated whites.[22] The upshot, Hochschild wrote, was that by the early 1990s, there were, in absolute numbers, about four million fewer poor whites and more than 680,000 more poor blacks.[23] Correlation is not causation, so it would be presumptuous to say that black retrogression in the 1970s and 1980s resulted from the implementation of racial-preference policies. But it's also improper for supporters of affirmative action to presume that all black gains have been due to these policies, given both the previous trends and the fact that the situation for low-income blacks worsened.

Racial double standards have had psychological effects as well. They've influenced how others view blacks and how blacks view themselves. Black accomplishment is met with suspicion by non-blacks, and recipients of preferential treatment can start to doubt their own capabilities. There's also the question of how much affirmative action has contributed to the academic achievement gap in K–12 education, which fuels calls for race-based remedies in higher education. How many black students didn't try as hard as they could have because they knew they would be held to a lower standard than their white and Asian peers? How many teachers didn't push their black students as hard for the same reason?

There is no disputing that black Americans as a group have made gains since the 1970s. The question is to what extent those gains should be attributed to affirmative action policies. One of the simplest ways to make that determination is by comparing black advancement in the decades prior to the 1970s with black advancement in the era of affirmative action. Yet advocates of racial preferences have showed remarkably little interest in doing that. Indeed, they often have gone out of their way to block such research or at least stop the results from seeing the light of day.

The litigation that led to the Supreme Court decision in 2023 banning the use of racial preferences in college admissions is a recent example of these tactics. But it is far from the only example. The case got its start nearly a decade earlier when Students for Fair Admissions, a nonprofit advocacy group that opposes racial favoritism, accused Harvard and other elite schools of discriminating against Asian American applicants. The lengths to which the schools went to shield from public view the relevant data on students who were accepted or rejected is revealing. Critics of affirmative action policies argue that they are unjust, counterproductive, and deeply divisive in a pluralistic society. Advocates argue that these policies are not only justified but essential. However, if advocates believe that special treatment for blacks is an unalloyed good that helps non-blacks as well by providing "diversity" in classrooms and the workplace, why all the secrecy in how the policies are implemented? Why not disclose exactly how the process works, including precisely how much weight is given to race and ethnicity when considering minority applicants?

When Students for Fair Admissions sought access to the documents that Harvard and Princeton had used to admit

Asian students, both schools objected. They likened their respective admission processes to "trade secrets" that, if revealed, would put the institutions at a competitive disadvantage in attracting students.[24] By this reasoning, the method of deciding what percentage of the freshman class should be black or Hispanic or Asian must be afforded the same confidentiality of Coca-Cola's soft drink recipe or an iPhone patent. The comparison is absurd. For starters, it's not uncommon for admissions officials to switch schools, presumably taking knowledge of admissions procedures with them when they go, yet they aren't sworn to secrecy about those procedures.[25] Nor does the claim that releasing data would compromise student privacy hold up, since names and other personal information can easily be redacted. Students for Fair Admissions argued that it simply wanted to know the number of Asians who had applied, their SAT scores and grade-point averages, and other information that the schools used to assess applicants academically. Ultimately, the courts sided with the plaintiffs, but it's telling that colleges have been so reluctant to provide such basic information, or at least reluctant to provide it to skeptics of affirmative action.

"Because the free flow of information and data in society is truly the lifeblood of academic research, it is more than a little ironic that higher education institutions have been extreme in their secretiveness about admissions and student outcomes," wrote Richard Sander and Stuart Taylor Jr. in their study of affirmative action policies. "Opacity is evident at every turn—particularly when data touches on race or racial preferences."[26] The reason to conceal such information, the authors surmised, was "no doubt in large part because of the large size of racial preferences and the poor outcomes of many students admitted with those preferences."[27]

Efforts to suppress both the extent of racial favoritism taking place and the evidence that these policies can have a negative impact on the intended beneficiaries go back decades. In 1991, Timothy Maguire, a law student at Georgetown who worked part-time in the registrar's office, discovered that black law students were admitted with significantly lower academic credentials than white law students. Based on a random sample, he calculated that the average white law student had scored a 43 out of 48 on the Law School Aptitude Test, while his black counterpart had scored a 36. The typical white law student also had maintained an undergraduate grade point average of 3.7, while the typical black law student had maintained a 3.2 average as an undergrad. If Maguire had discovered institutional racial bias *against* black applicants, he would have been praised as a hero whistleblower by liberals. But after Maguire published his findings in the law school's student paper, supporters of race-preferences were furious. The dean of the law school denounced the exposé as misleading but could point to no inaccuracies in the data that was cited and even claimed that "consideration of race was not a part of the school's admissions process," Maguire later wrote. Georgetown announced that disparities in qualifications was not a topic worthy of discussion and then "ordered the confiscation of every copy on school grounds of the offending issue of the student paper." To Maguire, who eventually obtained legal representation to avoid being expelled, the episode "revealed that a policy, whose fairness and wisdom are doubtful, has remained in force not on its merits but through the suppression of any criticism of its flaws."[28]

The racial gap in academic credentials at Georgetown was not limited to Georgetown. A similar disparity in black-white LSAT scores existed at the University of Texas law school, another highly selective institution. Nationally, the average LSAT scores for whites and blacks admitted to law schools was 36 and 28, respectively.[29] One study of college admissions data from the 1980s found that at the most academically selective undergraduate institutions, "African-Americans applicants enjoy an advantage equivalent to an increase of two-thirds of a point in high school grade point average (GPA)—on a four-point scale—or 400 points on the SAT."[30] Authors of another study wrote that "the edge given to minority applicants to college and graduate school is not a nod in their favor in the case of a close call, but an extremely large advantage that puts black and Latino candidates in a separate admissions competition."[31]

The point is not that law schools should base admissions exclusively on LSAT scores and undergraduate GPAs, but that those measures are highly correlated with everything from future grades and graduation rates to bar-passage rates and postgraduation employment. Likewise at the undergraduate level, standardized testing going back more than a half century has a strong track record of predicting future performance, which makes the large racial imbalance in SAT scores at elite schools troubling.

For decades colleges and universities have relied on SAT and ACT test scores to help guide admissions decisions, but in recent years the practice has come under attack. The opposition isn't new, but it gained considerable steam following the murder of George Floyd, when "antiracist" initiatives began to flourish. "The use of standardized tests to measure aptitude and intelligence is one of the most effective racist policies ever devised to degrade Black minds and legally exclude Black bodies," according to scholar-activist Ibram X. Kendi.[32] Critics reason that because white test-takers have tended to outperform their black peers, the tests themselves must be biased. That Asian students have consistently outperformed whites on tests that supposedly have a pro-white bent is rarely even acknowledged by testing critics, never mind explained. But whatever racial disparities are exposed when a seventeen-year-old sits down to take the SAT almost certainly developed much earlier in that student's life.

Kendi and other critics of standardized testing have argued that racial disparities in scores are rooted in socioeconomic differences among the test-takers. "The [prep] courses and private tutors are concentrated in Asian and White communities, who, not surprisingly, score the highest on standardized tests," Kendi wrote.[33] But if it's true that social class largely explains test results, how is it that Asians students from lower-income families have consistently outperformed black and white students from higher-income families?[34]

Kendi likewise ignores the role that cultural differences in attitudes toward school might play in student outcomes. But the scholar John Ogbu, who conducted a study of middle-class blacks in suburban Ohio, concluded that cultural differences could be pivotal. "None of the versions of the class-inequality [argument] can explain why Black students from similar social class backgrounds, residing in the same neighborhoods, and attending the same school, don't do as well as White students," he wrote.[35] "A kind of norm of minimum effort appeared to exist among Black students," Ogbu reported. "The students themselves recognized this"—they acknowledged studying less than their white peers, watching more television, reading fewer books, taking easier classes—"and used it to explain both their academic behaviors and their low academic performance."[36]

Racial differences in test scores are less a reflection of innate intelligence or class status and more a reflection of a young person's developed academic capabilities and cultural upbringing. Research has shown that professional parents talk to their school-age children for three more hours each week than working-class parents. By age three, a child from an affluent family has likely heard some thirty million more words than a child from a family on public assistance.[37] According to the US Department of Education, black parents on average have half as many books in their home as white parents.[38] Nor was it simply a matter of resources. Even wealthier black families tended to have fewer books than working-class whites. Another obvious variable in the achievement gap is the quality of education a student receives pre-college. Given that millions of blacks are relegated to some of the most violent and worst-performing K–12 schools in the country, it's no surprise that there are significant racial gaps in SAT scores. In large cities such as New York and Chicago, most students cannot read or do math at grade level, and black outcomes significantly lag white outcomes. In 2023, about 26 percent of all elementary school students in Chicago public schools could read at grade level, and 17.5 percent could perform math at grade level. Among white students, the numbers were 54 percent and 48 percent, respectively, but among black students those figures were 17.3 percent for reading and 7.8 percent for math.[39] Worse, these learning gaps continue in high school. And the disparities have persisted for more than four decades. As the psychologist Claude Steele wrote:

> Despite their socioeconomic disadvantages as a group, blacks begin school with test scores that are fairly close to the test scores of whites their age. The longer they stay in school, however, the more they fall behind; for example, by the sixth grade blacks in many school districts are two full grade levels behind whites in achievement. This pattern holds true in the middle class nearly as much as in the lower class. The record does not improve in high school. In 1980, for example, 25,500 minority students, largely black and Hispanic, entered high school in Chicago. Four years

later only 9,500 graduated, and of those only 2,000 could read at grade level. The situation in other cities is comparable.[40]

Kendi and other standardized testing opponents want to blame racial learning gaps on the SAT, but the test is revealing differences in a student's current ability, not manufacturing those differences. And scrapping the test, or minimizing its use in the college admissions process, does nothing to address the root problem. Exams aren't a perfect tool for vetting applicants to selective colleges—there is no perfect tool—but they are demonstrably superior to the known alternatives. In general, "subjective judgments of admissions officers do not predict students' later grades as well as a combination of the students' prior grades and test scores," noted one survey of the literature.[41] A study of nine private colleges found that the academic ratings of admissions officers—using subjective measures such as letters of recommendation and personality tests—had "less predictive power than the combination of SAT scores and prior grades, and when added to that combination, did not significantly improve the prediction of grades."[42]

One irony of nixing the testing requirement in order to achieve greater diversity is that blacks, Hispanics, and low-income students are among those who have the most to gain by keeping the requirement in place. Opponents argue that the tests underestimate the academic abilities of underrepresented groups and that high school grades are a better predictor of college performance. Among black students, however,

SAT scores have proved the better predictor, and those scores haven't underestimated how black applicants later performed in college. If anything, the test has tended to overestimate black performance. "Dozens of technical studies have addressed this question, and the results are surprising," wrote Professor Robert Klitgaard. "On average, test scores overpredict the later performance of blacks compared to whites" and the result "holds for colleges, professional schools, and job performance."[43]

Similarly, when the Board of Regents of the University of California voted in 2021 to end the requirement that applicants submit standardized test scores, it said the tests were biased against students from disadvantaged backgrounds. But research published in 2024 by economist Donald Wittman showed that the opposite was true. If the SAT and ACT were biased against low-income students, the score would underpredict their later performance in college. Instead, the tests tend to underpredict the college grades of wealthier test-takers, suggesting that the bias runs the other way—against the affluent. Wittman found that "SAT scores were more important than high school grades in predicting performance" and the "use of SAT scores in admission shows a bias in favor of students who come from socioeconomically disadvantaged families."[44]

The focus ought to be on improving the scores of underperforming test-takers, not banning the SAT or race-norming the results so that black students with lower qualifications than other students can be shoehorned into elite schools. In the late 1980s, the average SAT score at the University of California at Berkeley was 1181 for all students, but it was 952 for blacks and 1232 for whites. And although black enrollment at Berkeley was growing at the time, just 27 percent of black students were graduating within five years, versus 66 percent of white students.[45]

The black students at Berkeley were by no means unqualified to attend college. In fact, their SAT scores exceeded the national average of 900. At a less-selective school than Berkeley, where they would have been surrounded by students with similar academic credentials and taught in classes that moved at a pace they could handle, it's reasonable to assume that these students likely would have excelled at their studies. At Berkeley, however, they were struggling to the point where an overwhelming majority were pooling at the bottom of the class and some ultimately were dropping out. Studies have shown that black students admitted to elite colleges typically have higher SAT scores than the national average for all white test-takers.[46] The issue is whether they meet the normal academic standards applied to other students at the school, because those who don't tend to struggle. An analysis of students at the Massachusetts Institute of Technology, for example, showed that black students enrolled at the school had scored in the 90th percentile nationally on the math section of the SAT, but only in the 10th percentile among their non-black peers at the school, who had scored in the 99th percentile nationally. Consequently, a quarter of the black

MIT students dropped out, and those who did graduate found themselves concentrated in the lower half of the class.[47] One tragic legacy of the affirmative action era is that the number of black college graduates is almost certainly lower today than it would have been without racial preferences that mismatch students with schools for diversity purposes. When psychologists Claude Steele and Lisa Brown conducted a study of black students who attended a large elite university in the 1950s, they found that while "the grades of black graduates of the 1950s improved during the students' college years until they virtually matched the school average, those of blacks who graduated in the 1980s... worsened, ending up considerably below the school average."[48]

Unfortunately, affirmative action often doesn't receive the cost-benefit analysis that all policies warrant. The reason is that colleges and universities work hard to restrict access to important data that make empirically based assessments possible. "Scholars who have tried to do work in this area have had a tough time obtaining data, up to and including researchers from the Office for Civil Rights in the Department of Education," one study noted.[49] A political scientist and member of UCLA's admissions committee once voiced skepticism about the fairness of the school's affirmative action policy. When he requested data from UCLA, where he was on faculty, to study the matter, he was denied. Similarly, authors Richard Sander and Stuart Taylor reported that after a professor at the University of Arkansas at Little Rock had "expressed concerns that the university's use of racial preferences might wind up admitting students who would struggle on the bar exam, he found himself unable to get even elementary data linking admissions standards to long-term academic and bar outcomes."[50]

For supporters of affirmative action, however, accessing data on student admissions is much less of a problem. In 1998, William Bowen and Derek Bok, former presidents of Princeton and Harvard, respectively, published their widely acclaimed book, *The Shape of the River*, a full-throated defense of race-conscious admission policies at elite colleges. "No study of this magnitude has been attempted before," the *New York Times* editorialized. "Its findings provide a strong rationale for opposing current efforts to demolish race-sensitive policies in colleges across the country," and the "evidence collected flatly refutes many of the misimpressions of affirmative-action opponents."[51] The *Los Angeles Times* said that the authors "prove with fact, not anecdotes, that affirmative action works."[52] But "works" in what sense and to whose benefit? If the goal is to produce a racially balanced freshmen class, affirmative action "works." But when more than 70 percent of black students aren't graduating, which was the situation at Berkeley, can racial preferences still accurately be described as working?

Bowen and Bok argued that black students admitted to the most selective colleges with lower qualifications than other students fared just fine, and they insisted that academic double standards were indispensable to creating and maintaining a black middle class. In the years leading up to the book's publication, affirmative action advocates had been playing defense. In addition to incidents like the one at Georgetown, the Fifth Circuit Court of Appeals had ruled in 1996 that the University of Texas School of Law could not consider race as a factor in admissions. That same year, voters in California approved a ballot initiative that also banned racial preferences in higher education.

Bowen and Bok aimed to push back at this trend by showing that criticism of "race-sensitive" admissions, as they dubbed them, was overblown. "On inspection, many of the arguments against considering race in admission—such as allegations of unintended harm to the intended beneficiaries and enhanced racial tensions on campus—seem to us to lack substance," they argued.[53] But based on whose inspection? To make their case, the authors used a research database of admissions and transcript records from more than sixty thousand students at twenty-eight colleges and universities. That research project had been overseen by Bowen himself at the Andrew W. Mellon Foundation, which he headed after leaving his post at Princeton. Bowen persuaded dozens of schools to share their records with the Mellon Foundation, and the foundation allowed Bowen and Bok to use research from the project in their book. The problem is that all this cooperation took place with the implicit understanding that affirmative action policies would be painted in a positive light. So, based "on inspection" of the data by scholars already predisposed to support racial preferences, affirmative action "works." That's circular reasoning. The real question is whether *anyone* looking at the data—not just supporters of racial preferences—would reach the same conclusion. And skeptics of affirmative action have had a much more difficult time accessing the same data, if only to confirm Bowen and Bok's findings, let alone to conduct their own independent research on the merits of these policies.

"Undoubtedly the most valuable information thus far compiled anywhere for the study of racial preferences lies in the 'College and Beyond' databases created at the Mellon Foundation in the 1990s" under the direction of Bowen, wrote Richard Sander and Stuart Taylor, authors of *Mismatch: How Affirmative Action Hurts Students It's Intended to Help and Why Universities Won't Admit It*. The authors noted that many of Bowen and Bok's conclusions in *The Shape of the River* "are in sharp tension with other research findings using similar data." The problem is that the Mellon database is more closely guarded than Britain's crown jewels.

> Unfortunately, Mellon has erected barriers to other scholars who might critically examine Bowen and Bok's conclusions. Indeed—and incredibly—Mellon's explicit policy is to not make data available to check or replicate the results published in *The Shape of the River*. The databases are available only for academics who submit lengthy, detailed research proposals to the foundation, and these are then reviewed for approval or rejection. In effect, a scholar must go through the laborious

process of writing an academic paper, with blanks where the data analysis will fit, in the hope that Mellon's review committee will like the proposal enough to allow limited use of the College and Beyond data. To say this severely chills research is an understatement.[54]

When Sander and Taylor reached out to the State Bar of California for data on bar exam passage rates broken down by race and ethnicity, they were rebuffed at the urging of law school administrators. While it was already well-known that bar passage rates differed by race, law school deans didn't want the passage rates at individual schools to be publicized. "No dean wanted it known, for example, if whites and Asians at her school passed the bar more than 90 percent of the time but blacks and others receiving very large preferences passed 50 percent of the time or less," the authors wrote.[55] The schools were interested in black students for the purpose of advertising their diversity bona fides. What happened after those students enrolled was not a priority.

Nearly three decades later, *The Shape of the River* continues to be cited as the definitive assessment of racial preferences in higher education. When I debated a New York University professor in 2023 on the merits of affirmative action, he referenced the Bowen and Bok study as if it had settled the matter, even though, as we shall see, there has been considerable research published in the intervening years that has challenged the book's central claims. One of the most damning criticisms came in the form of a lengthy review of the book by the scholars Stephan Thernstrom and Abigail Thernstrom, who themselves had been denied data to study the effects of racial preferences. The Thernstroms began their critique by highlighting the self-serving nature of Bowen and Bok's conclusions. The authors "evaluate the effectiveness of the preferential policies for which they were primarily responsible at the two institutions they governed," the Thernstroms wrote. "But it must have occurred to them that it would have been acutely embarrassing if their evidence had revealed that racially preferential admissions policies had not achieved their objectives or had produced unanticipated negative consequences."[56]

The Thernstroms also took issue with Bowen and Bok for using an unrepresentative sample of black students at an unrepresentative sample of schools to make sweeping generalizations about the benefits of preferences. Among the twenty-eight schools in the sample, for instance, twenty-four were private and only four were public, even though just 9 percent of black students were enrolled in private four-year institutions. "Furthermore, even the small fraction of African Americans attending private schools were mostly at institutions with minimal admissions requirements and hence no need for preferential policies at all."[57] In the Bowen-Bok sample, 64 percent of black students had at least one parent who had graduated from college, or "nearly six times the proportion among all black college-age youths," and just 14 percent of blacks in the sample were from families of "low socioeconomic status," while the national figure for blacks was 50 percent.[58]

The more fundamental problem with the Bowen-Bok analysis was that it didn't compare outcomes of black students admitted to elite schools *with* preferences and those who were admitted *without* them. If you don't do that, you're not even addressing the core criticism of affirmative action in higher education, let alone refuting it. "The book's premise was that admitting black applicants to colleges and universities with lower qualifications than those required of other applicants has not produced the bad results claimed by critics of affirmative action," wrote Thomas Sowell. "The authors mobilized and displayed voluminous statistics, in an attempt to show that such students succeeded academically and succeeded later in life." However, the data showcased in *The Shape of the River* "were not about black students who were admitted with lower qualifications than other students. They were about black students in general in the institutions covered, *including black students admitted under the same standards as white students*. This much-touted study is *Hamlet* without the prince of Denmark."[59] (The emphasis is Sowell's.)

This failure to properly disaggregate the data was not an innocent oversight on the part of Bowen and Bok. They knew that separating black applicants who received preferential treatment from those who did not would run against their claims, which is what other studies, before and since, have shown. The graduation rate in the Bowen-Bok sample was about 80 percent for black students, which is impressive by national standards, but black dropout rates were also more than three times the white dropout rates, a differential that is significantly larger than the overall national gap.[60] If the goal of the book was a straightforward analysis of the efficacy of affirmative action, wouldn't it have been helpful to know the black graduation and dropout rates broken down by preferential versus regular admits? Bowen and Bok could have divulged that but didn't.

More evidence that the black students admitted preferentially were more likely to struggle showed up in grading. "The cumulative grade point averages (GPAs) of the black students at their twenty-eight schools put them at the twenty-third percentile of the class—in the bottom quarter, that is," the Thernstroms wrote. "Even the twenty-third percentile figure is deceptively rosy, because it includes many students who met the regular academic requirements for admission and received no racial preference—about half of the black undergraduates." If the authors "had examined the classroom performance of the half of the black student population that had been preferentially admitted, the picture would doubtless have looked worse. We are not given such a breakdown, despite its obvious relevance to the central issue in the book. They credit every academic achievement of African Americans who attended elite colleges to the preferential policies that affected only half of them."[61] Time and again, *The Shape of the River* used broad statistics to hide or obscure rather than to enlighten the reader:

> Nor are we told how many African-American students ranked in the top quarter or the top tenth

of their class, graduated with honors, or made Phi Beta Kappa. If the mean is at the twenty-third percentile, however, not many could have been near the top. This is another instance of the failure of the authors to supply relevant detail when it might have pointed to conclusions hard to square with their general argument.[62]

Further evidence of the harm inflicted on black students by affirmative action policies came from Peter Arcidiacono, an economist at Duke University, and two colleagues, Ken Spenner and Esteban Aucejo. They published an academic paper in 2012 on how racial preferences affect the number of black science and economics majors at elite universities. Arcidiacono and his coauthors discovered that among incoming freshmen at Duke who reported a major, more than 76 percent of black males intended to major in economics or the hard sciences, a higher percentage than among white males. Nevertheless, only 35 percent of black male students went on to acquire a degree in one of these majors, a drop of 41 percentage points. "For black women, the numbers are less extreme but nonetheless stark: 56% start in economics, engineering, or natural science majors, though only 27.7% has graduated in one of them," the study found. "In contrast, the differences between initial and finishing proportions in natural science, engineering, and economics are 5 percentage points and 17 percentage points for white males and white females, respectively."[63]

Remarkably, the study found that this gap in attrition rates could be accounted for by looking at entry-level tests scores among students. Like other selective schools, Duke admitted some black students with lower SAT scores on average than those of white applicants, but other black students who were admitted had academic credentials that matched those of the typical Duke freshman. The upshot is that those black students with test scores similar to the white average were no more likely than white students to switch out of the more challenging engineering, economics, and natural-science majors.

The experience of black students at Duke is a common one. A study of underrepresented minority students at twenty-three selective universities concluded "that race-sensitive admission, while increasing access to elite colleges, was inadvertently causing disproportionate loss of talented underrepresented minority students from science majors." The authors calculated that among students who intended to major in science, math, or engineering, 45 percent more of the women and 35 percent more of the men would have succeeded if they had attended schools where their academic credentials approximated those of the average student.[64]

Not only do these findings support critics of academic double standards who argue that these policies mismatch students with institutions, they also point to a less discussed but no less important byproduct of affirmative action: Those black students who don't drop out are often forced to switch to an easier major that wasn't their first choice. Had these same black students—who, recall, typically perform above the national average—matriculated at a school that better matched their academic credentials, they likely would have been able to major in economics or the hard sciences. "With the difference in course difficulty and grading standards between the natural sciences, engineering, and economics and their humanities and social sciences counterparts naturally leading the (relatively) least prepared students away from the sciences, affirmative action may be working to increase the number of non-science majors at top schools at the expense of science majors at less-selective schools," Arcidiacono and his colleagues concluded. "That is, minority students would be higher up in the preparation distribution at a less-selective school, potentially resulting in a higher probability of persisting in a science major."[65] Social-justice advocates complain about the dearth of black engineers, computer scientists, and economists, but a half-century of affirmative action has clearly contributed to that dearth. How many would-be black physicists or mathematicians instead wound up majoring in a less challenging field such as sociology or English after being lured to an institution where they were ill-prepared to pursue their first choice? White students are steered into schools that they are academically prepared to attend while affirmative action steers black students into schools for cosmetic reasons.

Some proponents of racial preferences insist that black students are better off muddling through a prestige college rather than flourishing at a less-selective institution, but empirical data and common sense suggests otherwise. At the end of the day, who is helped by flunking out of the more-selective University of Michigan versus graduating from the less-selective Michigan State University? Students at George Mason University's law school on average had higher law school admissions test scores than students at historically black Howard University School of Law. Yet an academic study showed that 57 percent of students at Howard Law, a school that did not use affirmative action in its admissions process, graduated and passed the bar exam on their first try. That figure was significantly higher than the comparable 30 percent rate for blacks at GMU Law, which did utilize racial preferences.[66] When the rubber hit the road in terms of graduating and passing the bar, how could you possibly conclude that black students at higher-ranked GMU Law received a superior education to the black students at lower-ranked Howard Law? How could you argue that GMU's use of affirmative action was doing anything other than stunting the growth in the number of black lawyers and, by extension, the number of black professionals? Clearly, attending a "better" school cannot be automatically equated with getting a better education.

In 2003, five years after *The Shape of the River* was published, another product of the Mellon Foundation was released. Stephen Cole and Elinor Barber's *Increasing Faculty Diversity: The Occupational Choices of High-Achieving Minority Students* explained how affirmative action had harmed the prospects of talented black students. Many of the best-prepared black students "are admitted to schools where, on average, white students' scores are substantially higher, exceeding those of African Americans by about 200 points or more," they wrote. "Not surprisingly, in this kind of competitive situation, African Americans get relatively low grades. It is a fact that in virtually all selective schools (colleges, law schools, medical schools, etc.) where racial preferences in admission is practiced, the majority of African American students end up in the lower quarter of the class."[67] Sadly, the authors noted, affirmative action also causes bright black students to doubt their abilities. "It is not at all surprising that academic performance in college should turn out to be an important influence on the decision to select academia as a career," wrote Cole and Barber. "If a student is not academically successful and has not received rewards for his or her academic performance, it would make little sense for that student to think of spending the rest of his or her life in a job where 'being good in school' is a prerequisite."[68]

The legal scholar Gail Heriot argued that it's useful to compare the Cole-Barber and Bowen-Bok studies. "In some ways *The Shape of the River* and *Increasing Faculty Diversity* are twins," she wrote. "They both contain a wealth of data, and in both books, the data showed that affirmative action–induced low grades were creating a serious obstacle to minority students' achievement. The difference is that Cole and Barber understood what they had uncovered and reported it in the text of the book forthrightly. In *The Shape of the River*, the data were ignored or misinterpreted." The reception of the two books is also worth comparing. "Unlike *The Shape of the River*, *Increasing Faculty Diversity* was barely mentioned in the press," Heriot noted. "The hardworking publicists for the Mellon Foundation were apparently on holiday. An exception to the media blackout was an article entitled 'The Unintended Consequences of Affirmative Action' in the *Chronicle of Higher Education*, which reported on the efforts of Mellon Foundation to distance itself from Stephen Cole. (Dr. Barber had passed away while the book was in preparation.)"[69]

The academic mismatch problem that is highlighted by race-preference detractors today was identified more than fifty years ago. And critics at that time likewise anticipated that the effects would by no means be limited to the nation's most selective schools. In a 1970 article about affirmative action in law schools, Professor Clyde Summers of Yale Law School said that racial preferences were legally dubious, and he lamented the semantic games being played by proponents. "The practice of preferential admissions, whether open and explicit or disguised with euphemisms, is plainly and simply a preference based on membership in a racial or ethnic group," he said. "As such, it immediately raises the most fundamental issues as to its legality and its propriety, for racial preference is but the obverse side of racial discrimination."[70] But the bulk of the article was devoted not to whether preferential admission policies are constitutional but the "antecedent question of whether it is prudent."[71] Summers wrote that the minuscule number of black lawyers was "disgraceful," but using preferential admission policies to grow the number was an "unreal solution." He warned that the top tier schools would be able to admit more blacks through affirmative action but that this would not necessarily increase the overall number of law students. "If Harvard or Yale, for example, admit minority students with test scores 100 to 150 points below that normally required for a non-minority student to get admitted, the total number of minority students able to obtain a legal education is not increased thereby," Summer wrote. "The minority students given such preference would meet the normal admissions standards at Illinois, Rutgers or Texas." Consequently, Illinois, Rutgers, and Texas would soften their standards to admit minority students who would otherwise attend schools in the tier below Illinois, Rutgers, and Texas. And so on.

> Thus, each law school, by its preferential admission policies, simply takes minority students away from other schools whose admission standards are further down the scale. Any net gain in the total number of minority students admitted must come, if it comes at all, because those schools whose admission standards are at the bottom of the scale take students whom they would not otherwise take. Because these schools have relatively open admissions for all who meet minimum standards, this would require their lowering those standards for minority students. In sum, the policy of preferential admission has a pervasive shifting effect, causing large numbers of minority students to attend law schools whose normal admission standards

they do not meet, instead of attending other law schools whose normal standards they do meet.[72]

Abandoning normal law school admission standards to increase the number of minority law students was "irresponsible, if not cruel," Summers wrote. The student admitted in such a way stood a good chance of ending up "confused, floundering and unable to keep up." Far from helping, "the preference given to a minority student seriously jeopardizes his chances of getting a good legal education. He is thrust into first year classes with students with much greater verbal facility and much more highly developed skills in manipulating ideas." His classes are "not geared for his needs but for those of students who make up the large portion of the class and who are prepared for the faster pace."[73]

Boosters of affirmative action at elite schools insist that these policies have played a significant and continuing role in expanding the number of black professionals. William Bowen and Derek Bok arrogantly claimed that minority graduates with advanced degrees from more selective institutions form the "backbone" of the black middle class.[74] This argument strains credulity. As discussed in earlier chapters, a significant black middle class existed well before the likes of Cornell began lowering their academic standards for black applicants. Moreover, according to Stephen Cole and Elinor Barber, the one hundred most selective colleges produce an estimated

4 percent of blacks who earn bachelor's degrees, while their less-selective counterparts produce the other 96 percent.[75] The evidence points to the less selective schools that don't use racial preferences—including the historically black colleges and universities (HBCUs) that were omitted from the Bowen-Bok study—playing a much more significant role in increasing the number of black professionals, then and now.

According to a National Research Council report, nine of the ten undergraduate schools that trained the largest numbers of blacks who went on to earn doctorates between 1992 and 1996 were HBCUs. The tenth school was Wayne State University in Detroit, also a predominantly black school that didn't use racial preferences in admissions.[76] The *New Republic* reported that in 1998, "for the sixth straight year," Xavier University in Louisiana, a historically black institution where many students are the first in their family to pursue college, "sent more black students to medical school than any other college in America."[77] The same article also noted that six of the top ten schools with the largest number of black alumni who go on to become scientists are HBCUs.

More recently, data from the Association of American Medical Colleges showed that "two historically Black medical schools, Howard and Morehouse, graduated more Black students than any predominantly White medical school in the country."[78] HBCUs today are seven of the top eight institutions that graduate the highest number of black undergraduate students who go on to earn science and engineering doctorates. They produce 40 percent of all black engineers, 80 percent of black judges, and half of all black physicians and lawyers. Supreme Court Justice Clarence Thomas's concurrence in *Students for Fair Admissions v. Harvard* noted that "Xavier University, an HBCU with only a small percentage of white students, has had better success at helping low-income students move into the middle class than Harvard has." The argument that racial preferences underpin the creation and sustenance of the black middle class is fanciful. It's an attempt by some to take credit they don't deserve for black advancement. The success of HBCUs in this regard also complicates the so-called diversity rationale for affirmative action, which is the claim that racial balance in enrollment ought to be a priority in higher education because it is somehow—it's never quite explained quantitatively—crucial to the learning process. The argument has never made much sense, especially given that students in much more racially and ethnically homogenous countries such as Japan and South Korea regularly outperform American students on international tests.[79]

Racial diversity may be pleasing to the eye and make for a more attractive college brochure, but it's long been evident that blacks (and other groups) are capable of academic success without a critical mass of white students around. More important, efforts to achieve diversity by lowering standards have coincided with slower rather than accelerated black upward mobility. "Instead of recommending that minority students go to the most prestigious school they can get into, high school guidance counselors should recommend that each student go to a school where he or she is likely to do well academically," advised Stephen Cole and Elinor Barber. "An HBCU may be such a school. Guidance counselors, in short, should try to reduce some of the lack of fit between the level of academic preparation of minority students and the schools where they enroll."[80]

In 1996, two years before *The Shape of the River* was published, residents of California approved a ballot initiative that prohibited public institutions in the state, including the University of California system, from choosing applicants based on their race. The result was a natural experiment in what a post–affirmative action era in higher education might look like. In 2013, the *New York Times* ran a front-page story on California's ability to keep enrollment diverse notwithstanding the ban on race-conscious admissions. Black and Hispanic enrollment had initially dipped, particularly at two of the most selective schools in California, UCLA and UC Berkeley. This is as you might expect would happen with preferences no longer in place and the racial gap in SAT scores. "California was one of the first states to abolish affirmative action, after voters approved Proposition 209 in 1996," wrote the *Times*. "Across the University of California system, Latinos fell to 12 percent of newly enrolled state residents in the mid-1990s from more than 15 percent, and blacks declined to 3 percent from 4 percent. At the most competitive campuses, at Berkeley and Los Angeles, the decline was much steeper." But the article went on to report "eventually, the numbers rebounded" and that "a similar pattern of decline and recovery followed at other state universities that eliminated race as a factor in admissions."[81]

The details of what happened after California mandated race-blind admissions were described in an empirical study by Richard Sander and Stuart Taylor, which shows that the ranking of the school is far less important to academic success than whether the gap in qualifications between black students and other students is large or small. The authors reported that after the affirmative action ban went into effect, there was only a 2 percent drop in the number of blacks entering the UC system as freshmen and 22 percent increase in the number of Hispanic freshmen. Meanwhile, the number of black and Hispanic freshmen "who went on to graduate in four years rose 55 percent." The number "who went on to graduate in four years with STEM degrees rose 51 percent." And the number of "UC black and Hispanic freshmen who went on to graduate in four years with GPAs of 3.5 or higher rose by 63 percent." A higher percentage of blacks and Hispanics also earned PhDs and science, technology, engineering, and mathematics (STEM) graduate degrees after the UC system ended racial preferences in admissions.[82]

After race-conscious admissions were banned, black and Hispanic enrollment fell sharply at UC Berkeley and UCLA— two of the most selective schools in the UC system. Yet it rose at UC Irvine, UC Riverside, UC Santa Cruz, and other less-selective institutions as students were redistributed to campuses where their academic preparation matched the school average. The results were higher enrollment, higher grades, and higher graduation rates for underrepresented minorities, including in the more challenging disciplines. Sander and Taylor also reported that "improvement in black and Hispanic performance was particularly noticeable among the best students." The number and proportion of blacks and Hispanics achieving high GPAs after preferences ended rose "at a much faster rate than for whites and Asians," offering more evidence that affirmative action policies exacerbate the academic achievement gap. After racial preferences were banned, "the entire distribution of black and Hispanic qualifications moved up relative to whites and Asians" and "a larger proportion of black and Hispanic students were able to compete at the highest levels."[83]

After California prohibited racial preferences in higher education, proponents made dire predictions like the ones heard after the Supreme Court's 2023 ruling in *Students for Fair Admissions v. Harvard*. President Bill Clinton, for example, said the California ban would "resegregate" universities.[84] That hasn't happened, but the fallout has provided yet more solid evidence that preferential policies harm not only non-preferred groups, such as whites and Asians, but also the intended beneficiaries.

SIX

Conclusion

After Affirmative Action

T he race scholar Shelby Steele calls them "poetic truths." They are racial narratives that minimize or even ignore objective facts for the purpose of advancing a political agenda. Social justice advocates and others who traffic in poetic truths typically don't do so out of ignorance. Rather, they know a given narrative is false, or misleading at best, but believe themselves to be acting for the greater good. For advocates of affirmative action and its offshoots—"antiracism," multiculturalism, "diversity, equity, and inclusion"—poetic truths are the coin of the realm.

An example of a poetic truth that gained momentum in recent years concerns race and law enforcement. Encounters between police and black suspects have received wider attention thanks to social media, which has given many people the impression that they happen more often, even though empirical data show that police use of lethal force has declined. In New York City, home to the largest police force in the country, police shootings fell by more than 90 percent between 1971 and 2015.[1] Social justice advocates, however, simply ignore such data. In 2022, a woman named Nusrat Choudhury was nominated by President Joe Biden to serve as a judge on the US District Court for the Eastern District of New York. Choudhury is a product of Columbia University and Yale Law School and worked as a lawyer for the American Civil Liberties Union's Racial Justice Program. When Choudhury appeared before the Senate Judiciary Committee for a hearing on her nomination, she was questioned by Republican senator John Kennedy of Louisiana about past remarks she made while employed at the ACLU:

> **Kennedy:** In 2015, you were on a panel at Princeton University. You said that "the killing of unarmed black men by police happens every day in America." Did you say that?
>
> **Choudhury:** Senator, I don't recall the statement, but it's something I may have said in that context.
>
> **Kennedy:** You think it happens every single day?
>
> **Choudhury:** Senator, I believe in that statement I was making a comment in my role as an advo-

cate, and I was engaging in rhetorical advocacy, as advocates do.

Kennedy: But do you believe that police officers kill unarmed black men every day in America?

Choudhury: Senator, I believe the killing of unarmed citizens by law enforcement is tragic, and I believe in that instance—...

Kennedy: I believe it's tragic too, but do you believe— and this is a really simple question, counselor—do you believe that cops kill unarmed black men in America every single day? You said it at Princeton.

Choudhury: Senator, I said it in my role as an advocate.

Kennedy: So, so when you say something that's incorrect, it's okay to excuse it by saying, "Oh, I was being an advocate?" What do you believe? Do you personally believe that cops kill unarmed black men every single day in America?

Choudhury: Senator, I believe law enforcement have an important and challenging job in this country...

Kennedy: I just think that's an extraordinary statement to make with no data to back up. No—none whatsoever. There's no basis for you saying that. And you knew it then and you know it now. How could someone possibly believe that you're going to be unbiased on the federal bench.[2]

Choudhury was confirmed and became a federal judge. But Kennedy was correct in noting that there is zero evidence that police officers in America kill unarmed black men daily, and it's hard to believe that Choudhury didn't know that. More likely, she simply didn't care, because claiming it was true advanced her agenda as an "advocate" for social justice. Nevertheless, black killings at the hands of police are statistically rare, and those involving unarmed black suspects are rarer still. A database maintained by the *Washington Post* showed that police shot 1,050 people in 2021, including 483 whites and 252 blacks. Thirty-three of those shooting victims were unarmed, including 7 whites and 12 blacks.[3]

Meanwhile, black homicides not involving police numbered more than 7,700 in 2019, more than 9,900 in 2020, and surpassed 10,000 in 2021.[4] It is not police misconduct but these civilian-on-civilian shootings, many of which are driven by gang violence, that are the real scourge of low-income black communities. Yet that narrative, however accurate, doesn't advance the left's political agenda. Therefore, activists like Choudhury choose to keep the focus on law enforcement, even if it means distorting the truth and smearing police officers. The political left reasons that the criminal justice system is racist because blacks are overrepresented. "Blacks make up less than 13 percent of the nation's adult population, but they account for about one-third of the combined federal and state prison rolls," wrote Manhattan Institute scholar Heather Mac Donald. Still, racial discrimination "on the part of cops and prosecutors is the only permissible explanation for that disparity; acknowledging the vastly higher black crime rate is taboo."[5]

Political scientist Wilfred Reilly, author of *Taboo: 10 Facts You Can't Talk About,* agrees that the narrative being pushed by activists doesn't comport with the facts, and that we can't simply wish away vast racial disparities in crime commission. "Black Lives Matter's claims about the frequency of unprovoked police violence specifically targeting African Americans are almost all demonstrably false," Reilly wrote. "In 2015, when the BLM movement took off nationally, only about 1,200 people of all races died during encounters with police. Only 258 of these people were Black, and, according to my calculations, exactly 17 unarmed Black folks were killed by white officers during the year." While it's true that the percentage of black deaths at the hand of police are higher than the percentage of blacks in the general population, Reilly added, that's not the relevant comparison because "rates of overall crime, violent crime, and arrests vary between races. The Black violent crime rate is at least twice the white violent crime rate. Adjusting for any of these differences—a very simple thing to do using modern 'regression' analysis—completely eliminates disparities in Black-white rates of police shooting victimization."[6]

Sadly, vilifying law enforcement can backfire in ways that do the most harm to low-income black communities. Studies have shown that police become less proactive—their contacts with civilians decline—and violent crime spikes when this happens.[7] Murders increased by close to 30 percent in 2020, the biggest one-year increase since 1960. Violent crime in general also rose from 2019 levels.[8] Some commentators blamed the COVID-19 pandemic for the phenomenon, but the trend predated the pandemic. Violent crime, which more or less had been steadily declining since the early 1990s, began reversing course in 2015, not 2020.[9] In 2014, eighteen-year-old Michael Brown was shot dead by a police officer he attacked in Ferguson, Missouri. Ample forensic evidence, grand-jury reports, and multiple Justice Department investigations cleared the officer of any wrongdoing, yet the incident, and the nationwide coverage it attracted, marked the beginning of a period of mass protests against police that culminated following the death of George Floyd in Minneapolis in 2020.[10] Post-Ferguson, there was a concerted effort by the political left to blame law enforcement for social inequality. Taxpayer resources were diverted away from police departments to appease activists. Sections of major cities were turned over to violent anti-police protesters. The public was fed a steady diet of nightly news stories about cops gunning for young black men. Camera phones and social media helped make statistically rare fatal encounters between police and black suspects seem commonplace, and the press expressed next to no interest in providing context.

Around the time of Choudhury's Senate hearing, the *New York Times* ran a story about the rise in gun violence in New York City and the impact on children and teenagers, forty of whom had been shot over a stretch of less than five months. Nowhere in the story was the reader told that the shooters and shooting victims in these tragedies are almost always black or Hispanic civilians. If cops had been involved, or if the shooters had been white and the victims had been black or Hispanic, we can be certain that those facts would have been highlighted in the piece. Yet aside from a reference near the end to a candlelight vigil attended by "mostly young Black children between 12 and 14 years old," race wasn't mentioned.[11]

By contrast, the same edition of the *Times* included an account of a fatal police shooting in Grand Rapids, Michigan, involving a man who was allegedly resisting arrest. By the third paragraph, the reader was informed that the police officer was white and the suspect was black. Next, we were told that the encounter "has raised questions" about "racial profiling," "excessive force" and "overpolicing." The use of the passive voice, suggesting that the newspaper itself is not advocating such speculation, was revealing. The upshot is that a news story about low-income minorities shooting at one another while young children were caught in the crossfire appeared deep inside the paper, and the story about a cop shooting a black criminal suspect ran on the front page—and was twice as long.[12]

It might be argued that police shootings make news because they're rare events, which is true. But police officers have killed many more whites than blacks in recent years, and these white victims rarely get the political and media attention that the black victims receive, which should raise eyebrows. According to the *Washington Post*, in the three years following the murder of George Floyd, the police killed 3,306 people, and just 1 percent of them were unarmed. The suspects killed by police during this period included 1,389 whites and 742 blacks.[13] How many names of those white shooting victims readily come to mind? Social justice advocates want us to believe that racist cops in cahoots with racist prosecutors and judges have it in for young black men. But advancing that notion requires them to all but ignore the high rates of black-on-black violence that can't be explained by white racism, and so they instead focus almost exclusively on the tiny percentage of black homicides that involve law enforcement. To indulge this thinking requires a suspension of disbelief normally reserved for watching superhero movies or reading fantasy novels. It requires pretending that something is happening even though it's make believe.

The narratives being peddled by elites such as Choudhury, and disseminated uncritically in the establishment media, are not only wrong but dangerous. They provided encouragement to the millions of Americans who demonstrated against law enforcement in recent years, sometimes violently. They help to explain why soft-on-crime policies are back in vogue, why police departments have trouble finding new recruits, and why the number of police officers shot on duty has been growing.[14]

Recent debates surrounding the supposed precariousness of black voting rights have been just as misguided as the discussion about race and policing. Here, again, the popular narrative—swallowed whole by journalists who ignore basic facts—strays far from the hard reality. After losing the Georgia governor's race in 2018, a black Democrat named Stacey Abrams founded an organization to fight voter suppression and subsequently became the progressive face of the cause. Yet by 2018 black voter registration and turnout rates in her state had surpassed those of whites. Her organization was a solution in search of a problem.

America has made great strides in black voter participation in recent decades, but you'd never know that listening to Democratic politicians, particularly when they are addressing black audiences. After Republican-controlled states passed legislation that they said was needed to address ballot security, President Joe Biden likened GOP officials to Bull Connor, Jefferson Davis, and George Wallace.[15] Yet black voter turnout had been rising since the mid-1990s, even as more states had passed voting requirements that the president insisted were "Jim Crow 2.0." Nationally, the black voter-turnout rate exceeded the white rate for the first time in 2008, when President Barack Obama was elected. It happened again when Obama was reelected in 2012, prompting the Census Bureau to note that the "increase in voting among blacks continues what has been a long-term trend."[16] It's true that black turnout dipped some in 2016, but only to the pre-Obama level. The decline almost certainly reflected apathy toward Hillary Clinton, the Democratic nominee, not voter-suppression efforts, because two years later, "all major racial and ethnic groups saw historic jumps in voter turnout," according to a Pew Research Center analysis.[17]

In 2020, Asian and Hispanic voting levels made history again, while black turnout was the third-highest on record for a presidential election. When minority voters these days are sufficiently motivated, they've had no trouble registering or casting a ballot. And when asked their views on voter-ID laws—as they were in surveys conducted by National Public Radio, Monmouth University, and others—large majorities of respondents, regardless of race or political affiliation, expressed support for such measures. Democrats and voting-rights activists aren't unaware of these facts, but they don't talk about them to avoid undercutting a voter-suppression storyline. If the goal of the GOP is to stop black people from voting, it's failing.

The positive national trends in black voter turnout are reflected in state data as well, including Southern states, where most blacks live and where black voting rights historically met the most resistance. According to the Kaiser Family Foundation voter database, black voter registration in the South has been higher than in other regions of the country and sometimes higher than the corresponding white rate.[18] In 2020, for example, black registration surpassed white registration in Maryland, Mississippi, and Tennessee, and the black-white difference was less than three percentage points in Florida, Kentucky, Louisiana, North Carolina, and Texas.

Turnout numbers tell a similar story. In 2020, blacks voted at higher rates than whites in Maryland, Missouri, Mississippi, and Tennessee. Democrats continue to assert, as Mr. Biden did in his Atlanta speech, that in 2013 the Supreme

Court weakened the 1965 Voting Rights Act to the detriment of blacks. That decision, *Shelby County v. Holder*, cited current black voter data as a justification for lifting the Voting Rights Act requirement that states with a history of voter intimidation secure federal approval of any changes to election procedures. "There is no denying," Chief Justice John Roberts wrote in the majority opinion, "that the conditions that originally justified these measures no longer characterize voting in the covered jurisdictions."

Since that ruling, black registration and overall voter turnout have continued to improve. A 2020 academic paper on voter behavior in the aftermath of *Shelby* concluded, "Despite well-founded fears to the contrary, the Shelby decision does not appear to have widened the turnout gap between black and white voters."[19] Still, liberals and progressives have no choice but to pretend that the opposite is true because acknowledging racial progress—however irrefutable—on this and other issues would undermine efforts to keep black people angry and paranoid, which has long been part of the Democratic Party's turnout strategy. Hence, blacks were treated to the spectacle of a president in 2022 trying to convince them that the franchise was as precarious as it was six decades ago.

The false narratives concerning policing and voting are subsets of a larger poetic truth regarding racial gaps generally and the role that a half-century of affirmative action has played in addressing them. The premise is that discrimination in the past and present is primarily responsible for today's racial inequalities, and that quotas and set-asides have been—and continue to be—essential to narrowing these gaps. "We expect that 25 years from now, the use of racial preferences will no longer be necessary," wrote Supreme Court Justice Sandra Day O'Connor in *Grutter v. Bollinger*, the 2003 opinion upholding the use of race in college admissions. But affirmative action didn't need another quarter-century to finally work its supposed magic because these policies were never "necessary" in the first place, and it had been clear for decades that if anything they were getting in the way.

In a landmark 1978 decision, *Regents of the University of California v. Bakke*, the Supreme Court ruled that race could be used in the college admissions process to achieve racial diversity on campus. Justice Lewis Powell, who issued the controlling opinion, wrote that the "guarantee of equal protection cannot mean one thing when applied to one individual and something else when applied to a person of another color." He also warned that "preferential programs may only reinforce common stereotypes holding that certain groups are unable to achieve success without special protection" and that "there is a measure of inequity in forcing innocent persons... to bear the burdens of redressing grievances not of their making." In the end, however, Powell seems to have overruled his conscience. He opined for the court that the Constitution allowed race to be used as a consideration in college admissions.

Twenty-five years later in *Grutter*, a case involving affirmative action at the University of Michigan Law School, the Supreme Court upheld the diversity rationale used in *Bakke*, and for another two decades schools were told that race could be used as a factor in admissions so long as it wasn't the determining factor, which is exactly what it became. One analysis showed, for example, that an applicant to Harvard with typical credentials had a 25 percent chance of admission if he was Asian. But if you left the credentials the same and simply changed his race to black, the chances of admission climbed to 95 percent. At other selective schools, such as the University of North Carolina, the racial difference in chances of admission were even starker.[20] Elite schools were openly flouting the *Bakke* and *Grutter* guidelines and using race as the deciding factor in which applicants were admitted. The *Students for Fair Admissions v. Harvard* ruling in 2023, which also struck down UNC's preference program, aimed to stop the practice outright and reaffirm the American principle of equality under the law. It's what Powell should have done forty-five years earlier.

In his majority opinion, Chief Justice John Roberts wrote that the Harvard and UNC admissions programs "cannot be reconciled with the guarantees of the Equal Protection Clause." Both programs "lack sufficiently focused and measurable objectives warranting the use of race, unavoidably employ race in a negative manner, involve racial stereotyping, and lack meaningful end points. We have never permitted admissions programs to work in that way, and we will not do so today."

But getting a majority of the court to finally agree that the Constitution means what it says may well come to be seen as the easy part. As legal scholar John Yoo wrote in anticipation of the ruling, "Even if the Court strikes down the formal use of race in college admissions, the campaign to enforce the Constitution's colorblindness principle will still have work to do. The history of resistance to *Brown v. Board of Education* suggests that universities will respond to a loss at the Supreme Court not by abandoning their goal of meeting some ideal racial balance, but by pursuing the same end through less obvious means."[21] In response to the *Brown* decision, officials in some parts of the South chose to close segregated schools, parks, and swimming pools rather than open them to blacks. Courts and legislatures repeatedly were forced to intervene, and they almost certainly will be called on to do so again in the wake of the *Harvard* ruling.

As Yoo predicted, demographic data on the first class of students to be admitted after the decision suggested that at least some highly selective colleges and universities were defying the court and still considering race in admissions. At Harvard, Columbia, and MIT, black enrollment declined, which was to be expected given that black applicants could no longer receive favorable treatment. But at other elite institutions, including Duke, Yale, and Princeton, black enrollment was flat and Asian enrollment fell, raising suspicions.[22] These are among the nation's most prestigious schools, where a minimum SAT score of 1400 (out of 1600) is generally required to be admitted. According to the College Board, which administers the SAT, among test-takers who scored 1400 or above in 2023, 25 percent (or more than 48,500) were Asian, and 1 percent (or fewer than 2,300) were black.[23] Edward

Blum, the head of Students for Fair Admissions, the organization that filed the case against Harvard, has vowed to enforce the ruling through more litigation if necessary. These selective schools will almost certainly test Blum's resolve.

The era of affirmative action didn't occur in a vacuum. It overlapped with a tremendous expansion of the welfare state that began in the late-1960s. Ever-growing government assistance programs became a lure and multigenerational trap for the black poor, while preferential policies fed racial resentment in the workplace and on campus, stunted the growth of the black middle class, and left the most disadvantaged blacks behind. Black marriage rates and labor force participation had been higher than those of whites for decades, but that changed after the 1960s, which saw soaring rates of black solo parenting, drug abuse, and violent crime—both in absolute terms and relative to whites. Describing the situation of the black poor in the 1980s, the sociologist William Julius Wilson wrote that "these low-income families and individuals are, in several important respects, more socially isolated than before the great civil rights victories, particularly in terms of high joblessness and the related problems of poverty, family instability, and welfare dependency."[24]

One reason antisocial behaviors became more common in the post-1960s era is because they became more tolerated and more lavishly subsidized by the government. Welfare-state programs that were created and expanded under President Lyndon Johnson's War on Poverty grew even larger and even more generous under his successor, President Richard

Nixon. According to a 2022 Cato Institute calculation, federal and state anti-poverty spending since 1965 totaled more than $30 trillion.[25] During this period blacks have been encouraged by civil rights leaders and Democratic politicians to embrace an ideology focused on victimization, grievances, and entitlement. Low-income blacks began to adopt counterproductive attitudes and habits that previous generations had rejected and strived to eradicate. Even more tragically, academics began to intellectualize this degeneracy instead of calling it out for what it was. Black Americans were "invited to enter into the larger society on their own terms," wrote urbanist Fred Siegel of the dominant thinking in the 1960s among intellectuals. "The schools, which had once helped set white-skinned peasants on the path to success, ceased incorporating dark-skinned peasants from the backward South into mainstream culture," he added.

> Discipline as a prerequisite for adult success was displaced by the authentic self-expression of the ill-educated. The newcomers, it was said, were not culturally deprived; they were "differently abled," more spontaneous and expressive. And after all, should a society guilty of Vietnam and racism be allowed to impose its values on innocent victims of its depredation? Like devout Christians getting right with Jesus, liberals struggled to get right with racism. They wanted to help blacks in the worst way, and that's just what they did.[26]

An academic paper on sexual behavior in low-income black communities in the 2000s included interviews with black teenagers about the sickening but not uncommon practice of multiple males "running trains" on girls. "In fact, 45 percent of the young men we interviewed (eighteen of forty) described having 'run trains' on girls (i.e., group or serial sex, often gang rape), and five of them reported engaging in multiple incidents in the last six months. Importantly, when young men described these incidents, they did not identify them as violence or sexual assault; instead, they constructed them as consensual." A thirteen-year-old boy named Frank told an interviewer:

> There's this one girl, she a real freak...She wanted me and my friend to run a train on her...[Beforehand], we was at the park, hopping and talking about it and everything. I was like, "Man, dawg, I ain't hitting her from the back." Like, "she gonna mess up my dick."...He like, "Oh I got her from the back, dude." So we went up there...[and] she like, "Which one you all hitting me from the back?" [I'm] like, "There he go right there. I got the front." She's like "Okay."

During an interview with an eighteen-year-old named Terrence, the following exchange occurred:

Terrence: It was some girl that my friend had knew for a minute, and he, I guess he just came to her and asked her, "Is you gon' do everybody?" or whatever, and she said, "Yeah." So he went first and then, I think my other partna went, then I went, then it was like two other dudes behind me...

Interviewer: Did you know the girl?

Terrence: Naw, I ain't know her, know her like for real know her. But I knew her name or whatever. I had seen her before. That was it though.

Interviewer: So when you all got there, she was in the room already?

Terrence: Naw, when we got there, she hadn't even got there yet. And when she came, she went in the room with my friend, the one she had already knew. And then after they was in there for a minute, he came out and let us know that she was gon', you know, run a train or whatever. So after that, we just went one by one.[27]

The author of the paper, Jody Miller, a professor of criminal justice at Rutgers University, was eager to contextualize this reprehensible behavior. "The sexual objectification and exploitation of young black women by black men is not only driven by a search for masculine identity," she explained. "The large presence of young men on the streets is in part a consequence of their exclusion from mainstream institutions such as schools and access to work in the formal economy." She described these sexual exploits as a bonding exercise that "increases solidarity and cohesion among young men" in poor black communities and said that other studies "suggest that gang rape may be particularly common 'in the contexts of broader structural violence, including profound marginalization and...depravation.'" She said that other scholars had "traced the sexual objectification of young black women to historical legacies of gendered racial inequality," including the "gross 'scientific' objectification of African women in the nineteenth century" and "their use as sexual and reproductive property under slavery."[28]

One problem with this analysis is that blacks living in the first one hundred years after slavery did not commonly exhibit behaviors that Miller is attributing to the legacy of slavery, even though blacks at that time on balance were significantly poorer and faced far more "exclusion from mainstream institutions." The attitudes and behaviors that Miller describes began manifesting themselves among the black underclass only after the 1960s. They are a legacy of the War on Poverty, not slavery and Jim Crow. "Until the 1960s, poverty did not entail social dysfunction in the black community," wrote Robert Woodson, a veteran of the civil rights movement. "In ten years of the Depression, when the United States overall had a negative GNP and nearly 25 percent unemployment, the unemployment rate in the black community was over 40 percent. Even then, the marriage rate in the black community was higher than it was in the white community, despite times of economic deprivation and racism."[29] Woodson explained that sending single mothers government checks to compensate for absent fathers diminished the role that black men played in raising their children. Thirteen-year-old sexual predators result from fatherless homes and too few role models to properly socialize the next generation. However well-intentioned, the end result of the Great Society interventions was a marked increase in family instability among black people. "Prior to this time, even in the face of Jim Crow laws, legalized discrimination, and a lack of voting rights, the black community did not experience the wide-scale despair and destruction that we witness today because of a strong Christian moral code of conduct, a conviction in self-determination and mutual assistance, and strong families and communities," Woodson wrote.[30]

William Julius Wilson made a similar observation in his own study on the origins of social dysfunction among low-income blacks. "Despite a high rate of poverty in ghetto neighborhoods throughout the first half of the twentieth century, rates of inner-city joblessness, teenage pregnancy, out-of-wedlock births, female-headed families, welfare dependency, and serious crime were significantly lower than in later years and did not reach catastrophic proportions until the 1970s," he wrote in his 1987 book, *The Truly Disadvantaged*. "In short, unlike the present period, inner-city communities prior to 1960 exhibited the features of social organization—including a sense of community, positive neighborhood identification, and explicit norms and sanctions against aberrant behavior."[31]

The legacy of the Great Society is a legacy of black social retrogression that racial preferences only made worse, mainly by undermining the self-reliance that historically has been so essential to rising economically. The Great Society helped to detach work from income and remove the social stigma of relying on public assistance. Blacks today who champion norms and decency and speak out against aberrant behavior are accused of racial betrayal and practicing respectability politics. Black leaders and intellectuals are far more inclined to make excuses, blame others for black shortcomings, and insist that ending racism must come before addressing black personal responsibility. Too many young people have come to equate self-destructive behavior with black authenticity.

The data show that blacks who do adhere to social norms are doing significantly better than others, black or white, who don't, which suggests that the continued existence of racism isn't the pivotal factor in black success. For more than thirty years, black married couples have had poverty rates in the single digits, and black married men have had a higher labor-force participation rate than white men who never married. According to the *Wall Street Journal*, in 2018 the labor force participation gap between blacks and whites virtually vanished, the first time that's happened since 1972.[32] A strong case can be made that decades of affirmative action and a more generous welfare state ultimately served as a drag on black progress. And the legacy of the expanded social welfare programs is not only fewer stable black families but also more violent black neighborhoods.

A 2023 academic paper from the Institute for Family Studies argued that family instability may be a bigger factor than economic conditions in determining the level of crime in a community. "Cities are safer when two-parent families are dominant and more crime-ridden when family instability is common," the authors wrote. Nationwide, the total crime rate is about 48 percent higher in cities "that have above the median share of single-parent families, compared to cities that have fewer single-parent families." Even when controlling for variables such as race, income, and educational attainment, "the association between family structure and total crime rates, as well as violent crime rates, in cities across the United States remains statistically significant."

Fathers, the authors noted, provide more than a paycheck. They teach their sons responsibility, self-control, how to carry themselves, how to treat women. They tend to be more effective disciplinarians, and their involvement in childrearing is linked to positive outcomes in the academic development of their children. "The presence of married fathers is also protective against school suspensions and expulsions, as well as the risk of dropping out of high school." Between 1960 and 2019, the percentage of babies in the United States born to unwed mothers grew from 5 percent to almost 50 percent. "Shifts from the late-1960s to the 1990s away from stable families have left some cities, and especially some neighborhoods, vulnerable to higher rates of crime, especially violent crime."[33]

There are plenty of single parents who heroically beat these odds and raise children who go on to lead productive lives. The public policy goal, however, should be to reduce the number of people who will have to face those odds. And that means calling out behavior that is objectively harmful to people and society in general. "Family instability and father-lessness collide with racial and economic disadvantage to create a negative feedback loop in black communities, hampering children's potential and perpetuating racial inequality," wrote journalist Kay Hymowitz. Citing research by John Iceland, a demographer at Penn State University, she noted that "differences in family structure are the most significant variable in explaining the black-white affluence gap. In fact, its importance has grown over time relative to other explanations, including discrimination. Unable to pool earnings with a spouse, to take advantage of economies of scale, and to share child care, black single parents have a tougher time than their married counterparts building a nest egg."[34]

Government programs are no substitute for the development of human capital. If wealth-redistribution schemes lifted people out of poverty, these gaps would have shrunk a long time ago. Unfortunately, liberal politicians and activists have little interest in addressing the ways in which black behavioral choices impact social inequality. It's much easier to turn out voters and raise money by equating racial imbalances with racial bias and vilifying those who disagree. Academics have also tended to shy away from acknowledging the strong links between family structure, child well-being, and outcomes later in life. The reaction to Daniel Patrick Moynihan's 1965 report on the negative economic and social consequences of fatherless black families was met with such vitriol that a generation of scholars mostly steered clear of the topic.[35] Those who didn't were denounced as racists or accused of blaming the victim. "For several decades, there was hostility, approaching derision, to any cultural study of the poor, including black youth," wrote the scholars Orlando Patterson and Ethan Fosse. "While it has become legitimate again to probe the cultural life of the disadvantaged, social scientists continue to tread warily, and one kind of cultural analysis remains suspect: attempts to explain social problems in cultural terms."[36]

In 2023, University of Maryland economist Melissa Kearney published *The Two-Parent Privilege*, a book that explores the connection between marriage and upward mobility. In the preface she described the pushback she received from fellow academics for taking on the subject. "When I have spoken with other scholars in recent years about my plans to write this book, the most common response I have gotten is along the lines of 'I tend to agree with you about all this—but are you sure you want to be out there saying this publicly?'" she wrote.[37] Kearney later elaborated on this point during a podcast interview, where she said that writing the book felt like taking "a big risk" professionally because her peers tended to avoid addressing the role of family structure in discussions of social inequality and looked down on those who do. "My saying it's not discussed is probably more reflective of the circles I run in, which is, you know, higher ed, academia, which of course skews liberal," she said. "And progressive, left-leaning conversations about kids' well-being and concerns about

social mobility—in those circles, in those conversations, I often find that this topic is met with discomfort."[38]

In 2023, fans of hip-hop marked the fiftieth anniversary of the
musical genre's creation. It would be difficult to name another
cultural phenomenon that has done more to mainstream and
popularize aberrant behavior. Top acts such as Jay-Z, Sean
Combs, and 50 Cent got rich trafficking in ethnic slurs, gut-
ter lyrics, and the ugliest stereotypes about black people. With
mixed success, black parents have tried to shield their sons
and daughters from the celebration of materialism, promiscu-
ous sex, drug use, and drive-by shootings that pervades songs
from some of the genre's most successful artists. The left-wing
academic and political activist Cornel West has defended
gangsta rap as "primarily the musical expression of the para-
doxical cry of desperation and celebration of the black underclass."[39] But the cultural critic Martha Bayles, writing in the
1990s, speculated on how the music impacted white perceptions of blacks and noted that it wasn't uncommon for a rapper's behavior to reflect his lyrics. "[M]y revulsion to 'gangsta'
rap does not stem from fears that its fans will start gunning
down cops," she wrote. "No, my revulsion stems from the
spectacle of young black men who are not brutal criminals
posing as such, in order to sell thrills to whites. Or, more dis-
turbingly, from the fact that rappers are now getting involved
in criminal activity—with the perverse result that being arrested, indicted, and convicted boosts both their image and

record sales. Sometimes police are the victims, as in the alleged shooting of two Atlanta officers by rapper Tupac Shakur. But most of the time, the victims are peers."[40]

One of Sean Combs's biggest hits was "Bad Boy for Life," which includes the lyrics:

> Bottles to pop, joints to rock
> Played the background, hand on my jock
> Holdin' my Glock

In another song, "I Need a Girl," Combs raps:

> I need a girl who'll...
> Damn near die for me...
> Pay my bail for me, make sales for me...
> Do twenty-five for me, nigga steal a pound for me
> Shorty probably blow a nigga to the sky for me
> And go and sit in a chair that'll fry for me

In 2024, security camera footage from 2016 surfaced of Combs attacking a former girlfriend as she waits alone for an elevator in a hotel. He takes the woman by the neck, throws her to the ground, and begins kicking her as she lies motionless. He then grabs her by her sweatshirt and begins dragging her away from the elevator. For years, Combs had denied that the incident occurred, though he eventually settled a lawsuit that the woman had brought against him. After the video went viral, he issued an apology on social media, explaining that his "behavior on that video is inexcusable." At least seven women and one man have formally accused Combs of "physical violence, rape, forced druggings and sexual harassment," the *Wall Street Journal* reported.[41] Combs was subsequently arrested, charged with sex trafficking and racketeering, and denied bail. "Combs and his lawyers have denied the charges," the *Daily Beast* reported in November 2024. "But more than 150 alleged victims—many of them men and boys—have since come forward, and lawyers have filed more than a dozen civil suits against Combs."[42] As of this writing, charges were still pending.

As previous chapters have documented, blacks of an earlier era were adopting the cultural norms of mainstream society and urging the next generation to do the same. Since the 1960s, however, adhering to traditional values has been equated with selling out, and black elites have been far too willing to intellectualize antisocial practices. Scholars pretend that aberrant behavior among blacks is normal behavior and not to be judged, while playing down or ignoring the reams of literature showing that such cultural traits are major impediments to escaping poverty.

"There is nothing wrong with black people that the complete and total elimination of white supremacy would not fix," according to the author Ta-Nehisi Coates.[43] Apparently for Coates, whose remark is more or less representative of progressive thinking today, black advancement is entirely dependent on the actions of white people. Yet this portrayal of blacks as powerless is belied by the success of previous generations of black people who surmounted far higher racial barriers than exist today by focusing on educating themselves, developing work skills, and becoming self-reliant. The abolitionist Frederick Douglass, who was born a slave, called on whites to remove "the barriers to our improvement, which themselves have set up," but he emphasized that "the main work must be commenced, must be carried on, and must be concluded by ourselves." Coates is waiting on white people to rescue black people. Douglass understood that black people must save themselves.

Even if opponents of affirmative action are mostly successful in keeping proponents from doing end runs around the Supreme Court ban, the black underclass will still have to shake off the effects of 1960s liberalism. For more than sixty years welfare state programs, through the incentives they provide, have abetted socially destructive behaviors and attitudes, while elected officials and their media allies have told black people that the resulting carnage should be blamed on racism. This welfare state indoctrination will be even more difficult to move past given the political left's growing deference in recent years to social justice warriors, "diversity, equity, and inclusion" propagandists, and other far-left progressives who now dominate one of the two major political parties, as well as the mainstream media and most of higher education. Affirmative action is ending but a new generation of leftist elites that include journalists, activists, politicians, and academics want to keep the welfare state mindset alive and well in black America. Worse, they are motivated by self-congratulation and impervious to facts and evidence that don't comport with their vision of how the world ought to work.

During oral arguments in the *Harvard* case, Justice Amy Coney Barrett asked lawyers for the school about the future of affirmative action policies. "When is your sunset?" she said. "How do you know when you're done? I appreciate that you're undertaking all those efforts, but when is the end point?" Eugene Robinson of the *Washington Post* wrote a column in response. "How about when the racial wealth gap is closed?" Robinson said. "What about when the mean SAT scores for Black, Hispanic and American Indian/Alaska Native high school students consistently are on par with those of White and Asian students? Maybe when we are a generation removed from the vast racial inequities of mass incarceration?"[44] Robinson doesn't consider that blacks were making significant progress in narrowing racial gaps on all those fronts prior to the implementation of affirmative action policies. He doesn't consider that the affirmative action policies themselves might be part of the problem.

DEI advocacy can be similarly unreflexive. The *New York Times Magazine* reported in 2024 that the University of Michigan had "poured roughly a quarter of a billion dollars" into diversity, equity, and inclusion initiatives since 2016, creating "by far the largest D.E.I. bureaucracy of any large public university." But to what end? The reporter, Nicholas Confessore, noted that on "Michigan's largely left-leaning campus, few of the people I met questioned the broad ideals of diversity or social justice." Still, "the most common attitude I encountered about D.E.I. during my visits to Ann Arbor was a kind of wary disdain." Professors at Michigan are trained in "antiracist pedagogy," according to the *Times*, and most students "must take at least one class addressing 'racial and ethnic intolerance and resulting inequality.'" Like affirmative action, these initiatives were implemented primarily with black students in mind, but clearly they have not had the intended effect.

"D.E.I. at Michigan is rooted in a struggle for racial integration that began more than a half-century ago, but many Black students today regard the school's expansive program as a well-meaning failure," Confessore explained. "Michigan's own data suggests that in striving to become more diverse and equitable, the school has also become less inclusive." Surveys of students and faculty reveal a "less positive campus climate" and "less of a sense of belonging" than before. "Students were less likely to interact with people of a different race or religion or with different politics—the exact kind of engagement D.E.I. programs, in theory, are meant to foster," Confessore wrote. "Instead, Michigan's D.E.I. efforts have created a powerful conceptual framework for student and faculty grievances—and formidable bureaucratic mechanisms to pursue them." Yet none of the negative feedback has led the school to rethink its approach. "Instead, it has redoubled its efforts."[45]

Affirmative action's defenders can likewise be expected to double down rather than rethink their approach, which is worrisome because preferences for disadvantaged minorities not only produce blowback but also serve to undermine the development of attitudes and behaviors that enable groups to rise economically. When you tell low-income black people that America's slave past has doomed them to failure, that the police are targeting them for no reason, that their behavioral problems are someone else's fault, and that they are entitled to what other people have without putting in the same effort and developing the same capabilities, you are not simply filling their heads with lies. You are also the increasing the likelihood that they and their own offspring remain low-income black people. Yet the people who push such dangerous notions have perhaps never been more celebrated in the academy and the media than they are today. If the end of the affirmative action era ought to be cheered, this latter development ought to be of deep concern to anyone who cares about the future of the black underclass.

ACKNOWLEDGMENTS

I am grateful to the Manhattan Institute, where I am a Senior Fellow and have been given the time and freedom to ruminate and write on topics of my choosing. I'm also indebted to the Thomas W. Smith Foundation, the Searle Freedom Trust, and the Bader Family Foundation, whose generosity makes my work possible. Many of the themes I take up in this volume were first explored in my columns for the *Wall Street Journal*, and I'm forever indebted to Paul Gigot and his editorial page staff for their support and encouragement. Finally, I want to thank my wife and children for loving and indulging me.

NOTES

Preface

1. Christina Pazzanese, "Harvard United in Resolve in Face of Supreme Court's Admissions Ruling," *The Harvard Gazette*, June 29, 2023.

2. Caroline Vakil, "Obama Says Affirmative Action 'Allowed Generations of Students' to 'Prove We Belonged,'" *The Hill*, June 29, 2023.

3. Lucy Hodgman, "Michelle Obama Speaks about How Affirmative Action Personally Affected Her College Life," *Politico*, June 29, 2023.

4. Dominick Mastrangelo, "Princeton Professor: Affirmative Action Will Lead to Segregated Higher Ed," *The Hill*, June 29, 2023.

5. Jelani Cobb, "The End of Affirmative Action," *The New Yorker*, June 29, 2023.

6. Aaron Blake, "Who's Okay with the Affirmative Action Decision? Many Black Americans," *Washington Post*, July 6, 2023.

7. Gerald Early, "Black Americans Have Always Had Mixed Feelings About Affirmative Action," *Chronicle of Higher Education*, July 19, 2023.

8. Sam Howe Verhovek, "In Poll, Americans Reject Means but Not Ends of Racial Diversity," *New York Times*, December 14, 1997.

9. "Race and Ethnicity in 2001: Attitudes, Perceptions, and Experiences," *The Washington Post*/Kaiser Family Foundation/Harvard University, August 2001, 22. https://files.kff.org/attachment/race-and-ethnicity-in-2001-attitudes-perceptions-topline.

10. Nikki Graf, "Most Americans Say Colleges Should Not Consider Race or Ethnicity in Admissions," Pew Research Center, February 25, 2019. https://www.pewresearch.org/short-reads/2019/02/25/most-americans-say-colleges-should-not-consider-race-or-ethnicity-in-admissions/.

11. Sheryl Gay Stolberg and Dalia Sussman, "Gay Marriage Seen in Poll as Issue for the States," *New York Times*, June 7, 2013.

12. Frank Newport, "Affirmative Action and Public Opinion," Gallup, August 7, 2020. https://news.gallup.com/opinion/polling-matters/317006/affirmative-action-public-opinion.aspx.

13. Section 10(c) of the National Labor Relations Act of 1935; *National Labor Relations Board v. Jones & Laughlin Steel Corp.*

14. Hugh Davis Graham, *The Civil Rights Era: Origins and Development of National Policy, 1960–1972* (Oxford University Press, 1990), 33.

15. Nathan Glazer, *Affirmative Discrimination* (Harvard University Press, 1987), xi.

16. Randall Kennedy, *For Discrimination: Race, Affirmative Action and the Law* (Pantheon, 2013), 18.

Introduction

1. Margot Lee Shetterly, "'Hidden Figures': How Black Women Did the Math That Put Men on the Moon," *NPR: Weekend All Things Considered*, September 25, 2016.

2. Margot Lee Shetterly, *Hidden Figures: The American Dream and the Untold Story of the Black Women Mathematicians Who Helped Win the Space Race* (William Morrow, 2016), xiii.

3. Shetterly, *Hidden Figures*, 20.

4. Shetterly, *Hidden Figures*, 95.

5. Shetterly, *Hidden Figures*, 24.

6. Shetterly, *Hidden Figures*, 29–30.

7. Shetterly, *Hidden Figures*, xv.

8. Stephan Thernstrom and Abigail Thernstrom, *America in Black and White: One Nation, Indivisible* (Simon & Schuster, 1997), 185, 233–234.

9. Robert D. Putnam and Shaylyn Romney Garrett, *The Upswing: How America Came Together a Century Ago and How We Can Do It Again* (Simon & Schuster, 2020), 203.

10. Thernstrom and Thernstrom, *America in Black and White*, 184–186.

11. Peter Bregman, "Diversity Training Doesn't Work," *Harvard Business Review*, March 12, 2012.

12. Frank Dobbin and Alexandra Kalev, "Why Doesn't Diversity Training Work?" *Anthropology Now*, 10, no. 2, September 2018.

13. Jesse Singal, "What If Diversity Training Is Doing More Harm than Good," *New York Times*, January 17, 2023.

14. Tabia Lee, "A Black DEI Director Canceled by DEI," *Compact*, March 31, 2023. https://www.compactmag.com/article/a-black-dei-director-canceled-by-dei/.

15. Lee, "A Black DEI Director."

16. Elisabeth Lasch-Quinn, *Race Experts: How Racial Etiquette, Sensitivity Training, and New Age Therapy Hijacked the Civil Rights Revolution* (Rowman & Littlefield, 2002), xii.

17. Lasch-Quinn, *Race Experts*, xiv.

Chapter 1: Ain't Misbehavin'

1. Renee Graham, "Rolle Plays an Enduring Role," *Boston Globe*, May 21, 1995.

2. "John Amos on Getting Fired from 'Good Times,'" *Vlad TV*, https://www.youtube.com/watch?v=30aFA0TmUOU, downloaded 8/16/23.

3. Donald Bogle, *Primetime Blues: African Americans on Network Television* (Farrar, Straus and Giroux, 2001), 204.

4. Bogle, *Primetime Blues*, 203.

5. Bogle, *Primetime Blues*, 202.

6. Henry A. Walker, "Black-White Differences in Marriage and Family Patterns," *Feminism, Children and the New Families*, eds., Sanford M. Dornbusch and Myra H. Strober (Guilford Press, 1988), 91.

7. Diana B. Elliott et al., "Historical Marriage Trends from 1890–2010: A Focus on Race Differences," US Census Bureau, https://www.census.gov/library/working -papers/2012/demo/SEHSD-WP2012-12.html.

8. Stephan Thernstrom and Abigail Thernstrom, *America in Black and White: One Nation, Indivisible* (Simon & Schuster, 1997), 185, 238–239.

9. Herbert Gutman, *The Black Family in Slavery and Freedom, 1750–1925* (Vintage Books, 1976), 455.

10. Walter E. Williams, *Up from the Projects: An Autobiography* (Hoover Institution Press, 2010), 5–6.

11. W. E. B. Du Bois, *The Philadelphia Negro* (University of Pennsylvania Press, 1996), 323.

12. Roger Daniels, *Coming to America: A History of Immigration and Ethnicity in American Life* Second Edition (Perennial, 2002), 244, 256.

13. Michael Barone, *The New Americans: How the Melting Pot Can Work Again* (Regnery, 2001), 21.

14. Thomas Sowell, *Race and Economics* (David McKay Company, 1975), 75.

15. Jason L. Riley, "Lessons from the Rise of America's Irish," *Wall Street Journal*, March 14, 2018.

16. Booker T. Washington, *Up From Slavery: An Autobiography* (Gramercy Books, 1993), 164.

17. Du Bois, *Philadelphia Negro*, 395.

18. Robert E. Weems Jr., *Desegregating the Dollar: African American Consumerism in the Twentieth Century* (New York University Press, 1998), 12–13.

19. Isabel Wilkerson, *The Warmth of Other Suns: The Epic Story of America's Great Migration* (Random House, 2010), 218.

20. Thomas Sowell, "Getting a Bad Rap," *Tulsa World*, September 26, 1996.

21. Grady McWhiney, *Cracker Culture: Celtic Ways in the Old South* (University of Alabama Press, 1988), xxi.

22. Thomas Sowell, *Black Rednecks, White Liberals* (Encounter, 2005), 6.

23. Thomas Sowell, "Crippled by Their Culture," *Wall Street Journal*, April 26, 2005.

24. Wilkerson, *The Warmth of Other Suns*, 291.

25. Thomas Sowell, *Markets and Minorities* (Basic Books, 1981), 69.

26. St. Clair Drake and Horace B. Cayton, *Black Metropolis* (Harcourt, Brace and World, 1970), 176.

27. Drake and Cayton, *Black Metropolis*, 45.

28. Gilbert Osofsky, *Harlem: The Making of a Ghetto* (Harper & Row, 1966), 12.

29. David M. Katzman, *Before the Ghetto: Black Detroit in the Nineteenth Century* (University of Illinois Press, 1975), 158, 160.

30. Roi Ottley, *New World A-Coming: Inside Black America* (Riverside Press, 1943), 182.

31. George S. Schuyler, "Jim Crow in the North," *Rac[e]ing to the Right: Selected Essays of George S. Schuyler*, ed. Jeffrey B. Leak (University of Tennessee Press, 2001), 53.

32. Davison M. Douglas, *Jim Crow Moves North: The Battle over Northern School Segregation, 1865–1954* (Cambridge University Press, 2005), 3.

33. Sowell, *Black Rednecks and White Liberals*, 46–47.

34. Wilkerson, *The Warmth of Other Suns*, 291.

35. Wilkerson, *The Warmth of Other Suns*, 289–290.

36. Thomas Sowell, *Ethnic America* (Basic Books, 1981), 80–81.

37. Howard M. Sachar, *A History of the Jews in America* (Knopf Doubleday Publishing Group, 1992), Kindle edition, 258.

38. Sachar, *A History of the Jews in America*, 261.

39. Evelyn Brooks Higginbotham, *Righteous Discontent: The Women's Movement in the Black Baptist Church, 1880–1920* (Harvard University Press, 1993), 218. Kindle edition.

40. Higginbotham, *Righteous Discontent*, 218–219.

41. James Baldwin, *Baldwin: Collected Essays* (Library of America, 1998), 644.

42. Steven Millner, "E. D. Nixon Interview, July 27, 1977," *The Walking City: The Montgomery Bus Boycott, 1955–1956*, ed. David Garrow (Carlson Publishing, 1989), 546.

43. Ralph David Abernathy, *And the Walls Came Tumbling Down* (Lawrence Hills Books, 1989), 132.

44. Rhonda Colvin, "As Trump Attacks John Lewis, Here's How Freedom Riders Broke the Chains of Segregation," *Washington Post* online, January 15, 2017.

45. Martin Luther King Jr., *Stride Toward Freedom: The Montgomery Story* (Beacon Press, 1958. Kindle edition), 165–166.

46. Jonathan Eig, *King: A Life* (Farrar, Straus and Giroux, 2023), 202.

47. King, *Stride Toward Freedom*, 156.

48. Ibram X. Kendi, *How to Be an Antiracist* (One World, 2023), 106.

49. Michael Eric Dyson, *Is Bill Cosby Right?: Or Has the Black Middle Class Lost Its Mind?* Kindle edition (Basic Books, 2005), 219–220.

50. Deborah Solomon, "Bill Cosby's Not Funny," *New York Times Magazine*, March 27, 2005.

51. Leon F. Litwack, *Trouble in Mind: Black Southerners in the Age of Jim Crow* (Knopf, 1998), 154.

52. Stuart Buck, *Acting White: The Ironic Legacy of Desegregation* (Yale University Press, 2010), 16–17.

53. John Ogbu, *Black American Students in an Affluent Suburb: A Study of Academic Disengagement* (Lawrence Erlbaum Associates, 2003), 198.

54. Buck, *Acting White*, 137–138.

55. Susan Edelman, Selim Algar, and Aaron Feis, "Richard Carranza Held 'White-Supremacy Culture' Training for School Admins," *New York Post*, May 20, 2019.

56. Kenin M. Spivak, "The Folly of 'Woke' Math," *National Review Online*, September 16, 2021, https://www.nationalreview.com/2021/09/the-folly-of-woke -math/.

57. Williamson M. Evers, "California Leftists Try to Cancel Math Class," *Wall Street Journal*, May 19, 2021.

58. Daniel Bergner, "'White Fragility' Is Everywhere. But Does Antiracism Training Work?" *New York Times Magazine*, July 15, 2020.

59. Peggy McGlone, "African American Museum Site Removes 'Whiteness' Chart after Criticism from Trump Jr. and Conservative Media," *Washington Post* online, July 17, 2020. https://www.washingtonpost.com/entertainment /museums/african-american-museum-site-removes-whiteness-chart-after-criti cism-from-trump-jr-and-conservative-media/2020/07/17/4ef6e6f2-c831-11ea-8ffe -372be8d82298_story.html.

60. Shelby Steele, *The Content of Our Character: A New Vision of Race in America* (HarperPerennial, 1990), 95–96.

61. Barack Obama, "Keynote Address at the 2004 Democratic National Convention," July 27, 2004. https://www.presidency.ucsb.edu/documents/keynote-ad dress-the-2004-democratic-national-convention.

62. Barack Obama, "Remarks at the Selma Voting Rights March Commemoration in Selma, Alabama," March 4, 2007. https://www.presidency.ucsb.edu/docu ments/remarks-the-selma-voting-rights-march-commemoration-selma-alabama.

63. Barack Obama, "Remarks by the President and Morehouse College Commencement Ceremony," May 19, 2013. https://obamawhitehouse.archives.gov/the -press-office/2013/05/19/remarks-president-morehouse-college-commencement -ceremony.

64. "Jesse Jackson: Obama 'Talking Down' to Blacks," Reuters, July 10, 2008.

65. Michael Eric Dyson, "Yes She Can," *New Republic*, November 29, 2015.

66. N. D. B. Connolly, "What Obama Can't Say," *New York Times*, February 7, 2016.

67. Jelani Cobb, "The Politics of Black Aspiration," *New Yorker*, March 21, 2014.

68. Ta-Nehisi Coates, "How the Obama Administration Talks to Black America," *The Atlantic*, May 20, 2013.

69. David Remnick, "Going the Distance," *New Yorker*, January 27, 2014.

70. David Axelrod, host, *The Axe Files*, podcast, episode 538, "President Barack Obama, June 15, 2023," https://www.cnn.com/audio/podcasts/axe-files/episodes /d1da1b16-d9a5-4b91-8397-b021016e0494.

71. Thomas Sowell, *Social Justice Fallacies* (Basic Books, 2023), 27.

72. Sowell, *Social Justice Fallacies*, 26.

73. Amy Chua and Jed Rubenfeld, *The Triple Package: How Three Unlikely Traits Explain the Rise and Fall of Cultural Groups in America* (Penguin Press, 2014), 41–45.

74. US Bureau of the Census, "Selected Characteristics of People 15 Years Old and Over by Total Money Income in 2020, Work Experience in 2020, Race, Hispanic Origin, and Sex," *Current Population Survey*, 2021.

75. Jemele Hill interview with Ibram X. Kendi at the Aspen Ideas Festival on June 26, 2019. https://www.aspenideas.org/sessions/how-to-be-an-antiracist.

76. Jelani Cobb, "The Politics of Black Aspiration," *New Yorker*, March 21, 2014.

77. "Respectability Politics Won't Save Your Black Life," *Ebony*, December 8, 2014.

78. Thernstrom and Thernstrom, *America in Black and White*, 235–240; Anthony Leonardi, "Black Lives Matter 'What We Believe' Page That Included Disrupting 'Nuclear Family Structure' Removed from Website," *Washington Examiner*, September 21, 2020. https://www.washingtonexaminer.com/news/black-lives -matter-what-we-believe-page-that-includes-disrupting-nuclear-family-structure -removed-from-website.

79. US Census Bureau, "Table 4. Poverty Status of Families, by Type of Family, Presence of Related Children, Race, and Hispanic Origin: 1959 to 2016"; Jessica L. Semega, Kayla R. Fontenot, and Melissa A. Kollar, "Income and Poverty in the United States: 2016," *Current Population Reports*, P60-249 (US Census Bureau, 2017), 45, 47.

80. Nicholas Eberstadt, *Men Without Work: America's Invisible Crisis* (Templeton Press, 2016), 72.

81. Lauren G. Beatty and Tracy L. Snell, "Profile of Prison Inmates, 2016," US Department of Justice, December 2021. https://bjs.ojp.gov/content/pub/pdf /ppi16.pdf.

82. Thernstrom and Thernstrom, *America in Black and White*, 140.

Chapter 2: From Equal Treatment to Equal Results

1. Patrick Healy and Adrian J. Rivera, "12 College Students on the Education System," *New York Times*, October 2, 2022.

2. Gallup Opinion Index, June 1977, Report 143, p. 23.

3. Hugh Davis Graham, *The Civil Rights Era: Origins and Development of National Policy, 1960–1972* (Oxford University Press, 1990), 454.

4. Graham, *Civil Rights Era*, 455.

5. Maria Krysan and Sarah Moberg, "A Portrait of African American and White Racial Attitudes," University of Illinois Institute of Government and Public Affairs, September 9, 2016. https://igpa.uillinois.edu/wp-content/uploads/2022/03 /Krysan-Moberg-September-9-2016-1.pdf.

6. Drew DeSilver, "As Supreme Court Defers Affirmative Action Ruling, Deep Divides Persist," Pew Research Center, June 24, 2013.

7. Paul D. Moreno, *From Direct Action to Affirmative Action: Fair Employment Law and Policy in America, 1933–1972* (Louisiana State University Press, 1997), 69.

8. Jennifer Delton, *Racial Integration in Corporate America, 1940–1990* (Cambridge University Press, 2009), 26.

9. Margot Lee Shetterly, *Hidden Figures* (HarperCollins, 2016), 6–7.

10. Terry Eastland, *Ending Affirmative Action: The Case for Colorblind Justice* (Basic Books, 1997), 30.

11. Andrew Kull, *The Color-Blind Constitution* (Harvard University Press, 1992), 19–22. Kindle edition.

12. Charles T. Canady, "America's Struggle for Racial Equality," *Policy Review*, January-February 1998.

13. Thomas Sowell, *Discrimination and Disparities: Revised and Enlarged Edition* (Basic Books, 2019), 74–75.

14. Thomas Sowell, *Civil Rights: Rhetoric or Reality?* (Quill, 1984), 70–71.

15. J. Harvie Wilkinson III, *From Brown to Bakke: The Supreme Court and School Integration: 1954–1978* (Oxford University Press, 1979), 31.

16. Richard Kluger, *Simple Justice: The History of* Brown v. Board of Education *and Black America's Struggle for Equality* (Vintage Books, 2004), 681–683.

17. Graham, *The Civil Rights Era*, 372–373.

18. Graham, *The Civil Rights Era*, 104–105.

19. Graham, *The Civil Rights Era*, 105–106.

20. Whitney M. Young Jr., "Domestic Marshall Plan," *New York Times Magazine*, October 6, 1963.

21. Graham, *The Civil Rights Era*, 106.

22. Lino A. Graglia, *Disaster by Decree: The Supreme Court Decisions on Race and the Schools* (Cornell University Press, 1976), 50.

23. Graglia, *Disaster by Decree*, 51.

24. Graglia, *Disaster by Decree*, 50.

25. *Congressional Record* 110 (1964), 4746.

26. *Congressional Record* 110 (1964), 11848.

27. *Congressional Record* 110 (1964), 7213.

28. Christopher Caldwell, *The Age of Enlightenment: America Since the Sixties* (Simon & Schuster, 2020), 22.

29. Andrew Kull, *The Color-Blind Constitution* (Harvard University Press, 1992), Kindle edition, 2516–2517.

30. "Now the Talking Begins," *Time*, February 21, 1964.

31. Stephan Thernstrom and Abigail Thernstrom, *America in Black and White: One Nation, Indivisible* (Simon & Schuster, 1997), 139.

32. Graglia, *Disaster by Decree*, 51.

33. Lino A. Graglia, "The Supreme Court's Busing Decisions: A Study of Government by the Judiciary," *International Institute for Economic Affairs*, September 1978.

34. Graglia, *Disaster by Decree*, 53.

35. Graglia, *Disaster by Decree*, 55.

36. Graglia, *Disaster by Decree*, 66.

37. Sowell, *Civil Rights*, 68.

38. Wilkinson, *From Brown to Bakke*, 117.

39. Thernstrom and Thernstrom, *America in Black and White*, 172–173.

40. Nathan Glazer, *Affirmative Discrimination: Ethnic Inequality and Public Policy* (Harvard University Press, 1987), 48.

41. Thernstrom and Thernstrom, *America in Black and White*, 425–426.

42. Alfred W. Blumrosen, *Black Employment and the Law* (Rutgers University Press, 1971), vii–viii.

43. Graham, *The Civil Rights Era*, 250.

44. Herman Belz, *Equality Transformed* (Transaction Publishers, 1991), 51.

45. Eastland, *Ending Affirmative Action*, 54.

Chapter 3: Before Affirmative Action

1. Derrick Bell, *And We Are Not Saved: The Elusive Quest for Racial Justice* (Basic Books, 1987), 159

2. Derrick Bell, *Faces at the Bottom of the Well: The Permanence of Racism* (Basic Books, 1992), 12.

3. Anemona Hartocollis, "Affirmative Action at 50: Successes and Regrets" *New York Times*, March 31, 2019.

4. Thomas Sowell, *Black Education: Myths and Tragedies* (David McKay Company, 1972), 92–93, 131–153.

5. Derrick Bell, "Black Students in White Law Schools," *Toledo Law Review*, Spring/Summer 1970.

6. Bell, "Black Students."

7. Bell, "Black Students."

8. Bell, "Black Students."

9. Bell, "Black Students."

10. Bell, "Black Students."

11. *Chronicle of Higher Education*, September 16, 2022.

12. Noah Feldman, "Supreme Court Will End the Era of College Diversity," *Bloomberg*, October 16, 2022.

13. Sherrilyn Ifill, "When Diversity Matters," *New York Review of Books*, January 19, 2022.

14. Paul Butler, "This High Court Will Doom Affirmative Action," *Washington Post*, January 28, 2022.

15. John McWhorter, *Authentically Black: Essays for the Black Silent Majority* (Gotham Books, 2003), 185–186.

16. Quoted in Robert E. Weems Jr., *Desegregating the Dollar: African American Consumerism in the Twentieth Century* (New York University Press, 1998), 10.

17. Thomas Sowell, "Three Black Histories," *Essays and Data on American Ethnic Groups*, ed. Thomas Sowell (Urban Institute, 1978), 18–19.

18. Thomas Sowell, *Essays and Data on American Ethnic Groups*, 17.

19. Thomas Sowell, "The Real History of Black Schools," *Long Beach Press-Telegram*, October 22, 2001.

20. Eric Foner, *Reconstruction: America's Unfinished Business, 1863–1877* (HarperPerennial, 2014), 96.

21. Foner, *Reconstruction*, 96–97.

22. Scott L. Malcomson, *One Drop of Blood: The American Misadventure of Race* (Farrar, Straus and Giroux, 2000), 209, 341.

23. James M. McPherson, *The Abolitionist Legacy: From Reconstruction to the NAACP* (Princeton University Press, 1975), 206.

24. Robert J. Norrell, *Up From History: The Life of Booker T. Washington* (Belknap Press, 2009), 35–36.

25. Robert Higgs, *Competition and Coercion: Blacks in the American Economy, 1865–1914* (Cambridge University Press, 1977), 120.

26. Daniel Aaronson and Bhash Mazumder, "The Impact of Rosenwald Schools on Black Achievement" (Revised September 2011), Federal Reserve Bank of Chicago.

27. Leah Platt Boustan, *Competition in the Promised Land: Black Migrants in Northern Cities and Labor Markets* (Princeton University Press, 2017), 40–41.

28. Boustan, *Competition in the Promised Land*, 50.

29. Joe William Trotter Jr., *Black Milwaukee: The Making of an Industrial Proletariat, 1915 to 45*, Second Edition, (University of Illinois Press, 2007), 81.

30. St. Clair Drake and Horace Cayton, "Negro Business: Myth and Fact," *Black Business Enterprise: Historical and Contemporary Perspectives*, ed. Ronald W. Bailey (Basic Books, 1971), 65.

31. Martha Biondi, *To Stand and Fight: The Struggle for Civil Rights in Postwar New York City* (Harvard University Press, 2003), 12.

32. Martha Biondi, *To Stand and Fight*, 29.

33. James P. Smith and Finis Welch, "Race Differences in Earnings: A Survey and New Evidence," Rand Corporation, March 1978.

34. Stephan Thernstrom and Abigail Thernstrom, *America in Black and White: One Nation Indivisible* (Simon & Schuster, 1997), 84.

35. Hilary Herbold, "Never a Level Playing Field: Blacks and the GI Bill," *The Journal of Blacks in Higher Education*, Autumn 2006.

36. Bob Zelnick, *Backfire: A Reporter's Look at Affirmative Action* (Regnery Publishing, 1996), 34–35.

37. Robert D. Putnam and Shaylyn Romney Garrett, *The Upswing: How America Came Together a Century Ago and How We Can Do It Again* (Simon & Schuster, 2020), 207–208.

38. Robert E. Weems Jr., *Desegregating the Dollar: African American Consumerism in the Twentieth Century* (New York University Press, 1998), 72.

39. Thernstrom and Thernstrom, *America in Black and White*, 195.

40. Ben J. Wattenberg, *The Real America: A Surprising Examination of the State of the Union* (Doubleday & Company, 1974), 125, 128.

41. Richard K. Vedder, "Four Centuries of Black Economic Progress in America," *The Independent Review*, Fall 2021.

42. Thernstrom and Thernstrom, *America in Black and White*, 81.

43. Michael Javen Fortner, *Black Silent Majority: The Rockefeller Drug Laws and the Politics of Punishment* (Harvard University Press, 2015), 41–43.

44. Michael Javen Fortner, *Black Silent Majority*, 46

45. Ben J. Wattenberg, *The Real America*, 131–132.

46. Thernstrom and Thernstrom, *America in Black and White*, 83.

47. Thernstrom and Thernstrom, *America in Black and White*, 233.

48. Richard K. Vedder, "Four Centuries of Black Economic Progress in America," *The Independent Review*, Fall 2021.

49. Putnam and Romney Garrett, *The Upswing*, 210–211.

50. Putnam and Romney Garrett, *The Upswing*, 211.

51. Stanley Crouch, *The All-American Skin Game, or, the Decoy of Race: The Long and the Short of It, 1990–1994* (Pantheon Books, 1995), 75–76.

52. Robin DiAngelo, *White Fragility: Why It's So Hard for White People to Talk About Racism* (Beacon Press, 2018), 149.

53. Yonat Shimron, "Ibram X. Kendi and Nic Stone Talk Antiracism with Middle Schoolers," *Faith and Leadership*, February 7, 2023. https://faithandleadership.com/ibram-x-kendi-and-nic-stone-talk-anti-racism-middle-schoolers.

54. Ibram X. Kendi, *How to Be an Antiracist* (One World, 2019), 160.

55. Kendi, *How to Be an Antiracist*, 11.

56. Randall L. Kennedy, "Racial Critiques of Legal Academia," *Harvard Law Review*, 1745 (1989).

57. Kennedy, "Racial Critiques."

58. Kennedy, "Racial Critiques."

59. Randall Kennedy, *Say It Loud: On Race, Law, History, and Culture* (Pantheon Books, 2021), 68.

Chapter 4: The Reparations Ruckus

1. "Black Manifesto," *New York Review of Books*, July 10, 1969.

2. Boris I. Bittker, *The Case for Black Reparations* (Random House, 1973).

3. Thomas A. Johnson, "Blacks Press Reparations Demands," *New York Times*, June 10, 1970.

4. "Reparations Move Deplored by Rustin," *New York Times*, May 9, 1969.

5. Jon M. Van Dyke, "Reparations for the Descendants of American Slaves Under International Law," *Should America Pay? Slavery and the Raging Debate on Reparations*, ed. Raymond A. Winbush (Amistad, 2003), 68–69.

6. John Conyers Jr. and Jo Ann Nichols Watson, "Reparations: An Idea Whose Time Has Come," *Should America Pay? Slavery and the Raging Debate on Reparations*, ed. Raymond A. Winbush (Amistad, 2003), 17.

7. Randall Robinson, *The Debt: What America Owes to Blacks* (Plume, 2000), 7–8.

8. Tamar Levin, "Calls for Slavery Restitution Getting Louder," *New York Times*, June 4, 2001.

9. "Public Attitudes on the Legacy of Slavery in the U.S.," Roper Center, February 24, 2016. https://ropercenter.cornell.edu/blog/public-attitudes-legacy-slavery-us.

10. Juan Williams, *Enough: The Phony Leaders, Dead-End Movements, and Culture of Failure That Are Undermining Black America—and What We Can Do About It* (Three Rivers Press, 2006), 68.

11. "Public Attitudes on the Legacy of Slavery in the U.S."

12. Allen C. Guelzo, "Who Owes?" *Tulsa World*, June 17, 2001.

13. "Blacks Can't Sue to Get Reparations," *Spokesman-Review*, December 5, 1995.

14. "Appellate Court Rejects Slave Reparation Claims," Associated Press, December 14, 2006.

15. Mohamed Younis, "As Redress for Slavery, American Oppose Cash Reparations," Gallup, July 29, 2019. https://news.gallup.com/poll/261722/redress-slavery-americans-oppose-cash-reparations.aspx.

16. Bianca DiJulio et al., "Kaiser Family Foundation/CNN Survey of Americans on Race," Henry J. Kaiser Family Foundation, November 2015. https://files.kff.org/attachment/report-survey-of-americans-on-race.

17. Coleman Hughes, *The End of Race Politics: Arguments for a Colorblind America* (Thesis, 2024), 92–95.

18. Charles Campisi, "The Myth of the Trigger-Happy Cop," *Wall Street Journal*, February 2, 2017; Von Kleim, "Researchers Find No Racial Disparity in Police Deadly Force... and That's Just the Beginning," *Force Science News*, August 8, 2019. https://www.forcescience.com/2019/08/researchers-find-no-racial-disparity-in-police-deadly-force-and-thats-just-the-beginning/.

19. "Race Relations," *Gallup News*, July 2021. https://news.gallup.com/poll/1687/race-relations.aspx.

20. Jennifer Agiesta, "Most Say Race Relations Worsened under Obama, Poll Finds," *CNN*, October 5, 2016. https://www.cnn.com/2016/10/05/politics/obama-race-relations-poll/index.html.

21. Williams, *Enough*, 84.

22. Shelby Steele, "...Or a Childish Illusion of Justice: Reparations Enshrine Victimhood, Dishonoring Our Ancestors," *Should America Pay? Slavery and the Raging Debate on Reparations*, ed. Raymond A. Winbush (Amistad, 2003), 198.

23. Gregory Kane, "Why the Reparations Movement Should Fail," *University of Maryland Law Journal of Race, Religion, Gender and Class*, 3, no. 1 (2003).

24. Brent Staples, "The Slave Reparations Movement Adopts the Rhetoric of Victimhood," *New York Times*, September 2, 2001.

25. Tamar Levin, "Calls for Slavery Restitution Getting Louder," *New York Times*, June 4, 2001.

26. Glenn C. Loury, "Should the U.S. Pay for Slavery?" *USA Today*, February 5, 2001.

27. Arthur Ashe and Arnold Rampersad, *Days of Grace: A Memoir* (Ballantine Books, 1993), 168–169.

28. Ashe and Rampersad, *Days of Grace*, 170.

29. David North and Thomas Mackaman, "An Interview with Political Scientist Adolph Reed Jr. on the New York Times' 1619 Project," *The New York Times' 1619 Project and the Racialist Falsification of History: Essays and Interviews*, (Mehring Books, 2021), 133.

30. Linda Qiu, "Paying for the Sins of Slavery," *Tampa Bay Times*, January 31, 2016.

31. Ta-Nehisi Coates, "'Better Is Good': Obama on Reparations, Civil Rights, and the Art of the Possible," *The Atlantic*, December 21, 2016. https://www.theatlantic.com/politics/archive/2016/12/ta-nehisi-coates-obama-transcript-ii/511133/.

32. Peter Wood, *1620: A Critical Response to the 1619 Project* (Encounter Books, 2020), 171–172.

33. Ta-Nehisi Coates, "The Case for Reparations," *The Atlantic*, June 2014.

34. Jake Silverstein, "1619," *New York Times Magazine*, August 18, 2019.

35. Nikole Hannah-Jones, "Our Founding Ideals of Liberty and Equality Were False When They Were Written," *New York Times Magazine*, August 18, 2019.

36. Nikole Hannah-Jones, "What Is Owed," *New York Times Magazine*, June 30, 2020.

37. David North and Thomas Mackaman, *The New York Times' 1619 Project*, 126–127.

38. John McWhorter, *Woke Racism: How a New Religion Has Betrayed Black America* (Portfolio, 2021), 72.

39. Jordan Michael Smith, "The Education of Ta-Nehisi Coates," *Chronicle of Higher Education*, October 2, 2017.

40. Becket Adams, "1619 Project Founder Claims Her Project Is Simply an 'Origin Story,' Not History," *Washington Examiner*, July 28, 2020.

41. Elliot Kaufman, "The '1619 Project' Gets Schooled," *Wall Street Journal*, December 16, 2019.

42. Peter Novick, *That Noble Dream: The "Objectivity Question" and the American Historical Profession* (Cambridge University Press, 1988), 475.

43. "How the 1619 Project Came Together," *New York Times Magazine*, August 18, 2019.

44. Leslie M. Harris, "I Helped Fact-Check the 1619 Project. The Times Ignored Me," *Politico*, March 6, 2020.

45. "Historian Gordon Wood Responds to the New York Times' Defense of the 1619 Project," *World Socialist Web Site*, December 24, 2019. https://www.wsws.org/en/articles/2019/12/24/nytr-d24.html.

46. Anita Bhole, "Woke Disney Is Slammed for the 1619 Project," *Daily Mail*, January 30, 2023. https://www.dailymail.co.uk/news/article-11693831/Woke-Disney-slammed-1619-Project-Hulu-viewers-boycott-service.html.

47. John Murawski, "Disputed NY Times '1619 Project' Already Shaping Schoolkids' Minds on Race," *RealClearInvestigations*, January 31, 2020. https://www.realclearinvestigations.com/articles/2020/01/31/disputed_ny_times_1619_project_is_already_shaping_kids_minds_on_race_bias_122192.html.

48. Will Potter, "NYT 1619 Project Is Slammed," *Daily Mail*, June 6, 2023. https://www.dailymail.co.uk/news/article-12166457/NYTs-1619-Project-slammed-pushing-reparations-math-high-school-course-children.html.

49. Thomas Sowell, *Preferential Policies: An International Perspective* (Quill, 1990), 148.

50. David North and Thomas Mackaman, *The New York Times' 1619 Project and the Racialist Falsification of History*, 132.

51. Thomas Sowell, *Black Rednecks and White Liberals* (Encounter Books, 2005), 113.

52. Thomas Sowell, *Race and Culture: A World View* (Basic Books, 1994), 186–190.

53. Hugh Thomas, *The Slave Trade: The Story of the Atlantic Slave Trade— 1440–1870* (Simon & Schuster, 1997), 370.

54. Orlando Patterson, *Slavery and Social Death: A Comparative Study* (Harvard University Press, 1982), 159.

55. Peter Wood, *1620*, 16–17.

56. North and Mackaman, *The New York Times' 1619 Project*, 109.

57. Patterson, *Slavery and Social Death*, vii.

58. Thomas, *The Slave Trade*, 180–181.

59. Sowell, *Black Rednecks and White Liberals*, 145.

60. Hannah-Jones, "Our Founding Ideals of Liberty and Equality."

61. Allen C. Guelzo, "The 1619 Project's Outrageous, Lying Slander of Abe Lincoln," *New York Post*, March 3, 2020.

62. Sean Wilentz, "A Matter of Facts," *The Atlantic*, January 22, 2020.

63. North and Mackaman, *The New York Times' 1619 Project*, 83.

64. Hannah-Jones, "Our Founding Ideals of Liberty and Equality."

65. North and Mackaman, *The New York Times' 1619 Project*, 86.

66. Allen C. Guelzo, "Who Owes?" *Tulsa World*, June 17, 2001.

67. Larry Koger, *Black Slaveowners: Free Black Masters in South Carolina* (University of South Carolina Press, 1985). See also, Ira Berlin, *Slaves without Masters: The Free Negro in the Antebellum South* (The New Press, 2007), 124.

68. Karl Zinsmeister, "Has the Debt Been Paid?" *American Enterprise*, July 1, 2001.

69. Ta-Nehisi Coates, "The Case for Considering Reparations," *The Atlantic*, January 27, 2016. https://www.theatlantic.com/politics/archive/2016/01/tanehisi -coates-reparations/427041/.

70. Richard K. Vedder, "*Time on the Cross* at Fifty," *The Independent Review*, Spring 2024, 673–681.

71. Olivia Paschal and Madeleine Carlisle, "Read Ta-Nehisi Coates's Testimony on Reparations," *The Atlantic*, June 19, 2019.

72. Wilfred M. McClay, "How the New York Times Is Distorting American History," *Commentary Magazine*, October 2019.

73. Matthew Desmond, "In Order to Understand the Brutality of American Capitalism, You Have to Start on the Plantation," *New York Times Magazine*, August 18, 2019.

74. Deirdre Nansen McCloskey, "Slavery Did Not Make America Rich," *Reason*, August/September 2018.

75. Phillip W. Magness, *The 1619 Project: A Critique* (American Institute for Economic Research, 2020), 8–9.

76. Thomas Sowell, *Conquests and Cultures: An International History* (Basic Books, 1998), 167–168.

77. Thomas Sowell, *Race and Economics* (David McKay Company, 1975), 7.

78. Berlin, *Slaves Without Masters*, 184.

79. Thomas Sowell, *Race and Economics*, 8.

80. Paschal and Carlisle, "Read Ta-Nehisi Coates's Testimony."

81. Rakesh Kochhar and Mohamad Moslimani, "Wealth Surged During the Pandemic, but Debt Endures for Poorer Black and Hispanic Families," *Pew*

Research Center, December 4, 2023. https://www.pewresearch.org/race-and-eth nicity/2023/12/04/wealth-surged-in-the-pandemic-but-debt-endures-for-poorer -black-and-hispanic-families/.

82. John Elflein, "Maternal Mortality Rate in the United States from 2018 to 2022 by Race/Ethnicity," *Statista Research Department*, May 13, 2024. https://www .statista.com/statistics/1240107/us-maternal-mortality-rates-by-ethnicity/.

83. Stanley Goldfarb, MD, *Take Two Aspirin and Call Me by My Pronouns* (Bombardier Books, 2022), 65.

84. Randall Kennedy, *Race, Crime and the Law* (Pantheon Books, 1997), 20.

85. William J. Stuntz, *The Collapse of American Criminal Justice* (The Belknap Press, 2011), 21.

86. Stephen Baskerville, "Is There Really a Fatherhood Crisis?" *The Independent Review*, Spring 2004.

87. David S. Landes, *The Wealth and Poverty of Nations: Why Some Are So Rich and Some So Poor* (W. W. Norton & Company, 1999), 6.

88. Myron Weiner, "The Pursuit of Ethnic Inequalities Through Preferential Policies: A Comparative Public Policy Perspective," in Robert B. Goldmann and A. Jeyaratnam Wilson, eds., *From Independence to Statehood* (Francis Pinter, 1984), 64.

89. Donald L. Horowitz, *Ethnic Groups in Conflict* (University of California Press, 2000), 677.

90. US Bureau of the Census, "Selected Population Profile in the United States," *2019 American Community Survey*, 1-Year Estimates, Table S0201.

91. US Bureau of the Census, "Selected Population Profile."

92. US Bureau of the Census, "Per Capita Income in the Past 12 Months (in 2022 Inflation-Adjusted Dollars)," American Community Survey B19301D https://data.census.gov/table/ACSDT1Y2022.B19301D?q=B19301D:%20Per%20 Capita%20Income%20in%20the%20Past%2012%20Months%20(in%202022%20 Inflation-Adjusted%20Dollars)%20(Asian%20Alone).

93. Amy Chua and Jed Rubenfeld, *The Triple Package: How Three Unlikely Traits Explain the Rise and Fall of Cultural Groups in America* (Penguin Books, 2015), 46–47, 103.

94. Abigail Thernstrom and Stephan Thernstrom, *No Excuses: Closing the Racial Gap in Learning* (Simon & Schuster Paperbacks, 2003), 93.

95. "Civil Rights and the Mortgage Crisis," *United States Commission on Civil Rights*, September 2009, 53.

96. Thernstrom and Thernstrom, *No Excuses*, 138.

97. Nicholas Zill and Brad Wilcox, "The Black-White Divide in Suspensions: What Is the Role of Family?" *Institute for Family Studies*, November 19, 2019. https://ifstudies.org/blog/the-black-white-divide-in-suspensions-what-is-the -role-of-family.

98. Van C. Tran, "More Than Just Black," in Orlando Patterson with Ethan Fosse, eds., *The Cultural Matrix: Understanding Black Youth* (Harvard University Press, 2015), 252–260.

99. John Mollenkopf, "Trajectories for the Immigrant Second Generation in New York City," *Federal Reserve Bank of New York Economic Policy Review*, December 2005.

100. Steve Inskeep interview with Kamala Harris, *Morning Edition*, National Public Radio, March 14, 2019. https://www.npr.org/2019/03/14/703299534/sen -kamala-harris-on-reparations.

101. Coleman Hughes, *The End of Race Politics*, 136.

102. See, for example, William J. Stuntz, *The Collapse of American Criminal Justice*, 21, 37; Kay S. Hymowitz, "The Black Family: 40 Years of Lies," *City Journal*, Summer 2005; "Historical Statistics of the United States: Colonial Times to 1970," US Bureau of the Census (Government Printing Office, 1975), Part I, 135.

103. Kenneth T. Jackson, *Crabgrass Frontier: The Suburbanization of the United States* (Oxford University Press, 1985), 205.

104. Price V. Fishback, Jessica LaVoice, Allison Shertzer and Randall Walsh, "The HOLC Maps: How Race and Poverty Influenced Real Estate Professionals' Evaluation of Lending Risk in the 1930s," *National Bureau of Economic Research*, October 2021. https://www.nber.org/papers/w28146.

105. Price V. Fishback, Jessica LaVoice, Allison Shertzer and Randall Walsh, "The HOLC Maps."

106. Price V. Fishback, Jessica LaVoice, Allison Shertzer and Randall Walsh, "The HOLC Maps."

107. Price V. Fishback, Jessica LaVoice, Allison Shertzer and Randall Walsh, "The HOLC Maps."

108. William J. Collins and Robert A. Margo, "Race and Home Ownership from the Civil War to the Present," *National Bureau of Economic Research*, January 2011. https://www.nber.org/system/files/working_papers/w16665/w16665.pdf.

Chapter 5: The Affirmative Action Era

1. Thomas Sowell, *A Personal Odyssey* (The Free Press, 2000), 247.

2. Sowell, *A Personal Odyssey*, 248.

3. Walter E. Williams, *Up from the Projects* (Hoover Institution Press, 2010), 110.

4. Sowell, *A Personal Odyssey*, 306.

5. Clarence Thomas, *My Grandfather's Son* (Harper, 2007), 86–87.

6. Vincent D. Rougeau, "Clarence Thomas Was a Beneficiary of Race-Based Admissions at My School," *Boston Globe*, May 29, 2023.

7. Thomas, *My Grandfather's Son*, 49.

8. David G. Savage, "Justice Thomas Scorns Media, Affirmative Action in Interview," *Los Angeles Times*, March 3, 2007.

9. Thomas, *My Grandfather's Son*, 64.

10. "Supreme Mystery," *Newsweek*, September 15, 1991.

11. Neil A. Lewis, "On Thomas's Climb, Ambivalence About Issue of Affirmative Action," *New York Times*, July 14, 1991.

12. Lou Ferleger and Jay R. Mandle, "African Americans and the Future of the U.S. Economy," *Trotter Review*, 5, no. 1, art. 2, 1991.

13. Ferleger and Mandle, "African Americans and the Future."

14. Patrick Bayer and Kerwin Kofi Charles, "Divergent Paths: Structural Change, Economic Rank, and the Evolution of Black-White Earnings Differences, 1940–2014," Working Paper 22797 (National Bureau of Economic Research, September 2017). https://www.nber.org/system/files/working_papers/w22797/w22797.pdf.

15. Robert A. Margo, "Obama, Katrina, and the Persistence of Racial Inequality," Working Paper 21933 (National Bureau of Economic Research, January 2016), https://www.nber.org/system/files/working_papers/w21933/w21933.pdf.

16. Bob Zelnick, *Backfire: A Reporter's Look at Affirmative Action* (Regnery Publishing, 1996), 30.

17. Zelnick, *Backfire*, 31.

18. Stephan Thernstrom and Abigail Thernstrom, *America in Black and White: One Nation, Indivisible* (Simon & Schuster, 1997), 233.

19. Glenn C. Loury, "On the Need for Moral Leadership in the Black Community," *New Perspectives* (US Civil Rights Commission), 16, no. 1, summer 1984.

20. Jennifer L. Hochschild, *Facing Up to the American Dream: Race, Class, and the Soul of the Nation* (Princeton University Press, 1995), 45.

21. Sean F. Reardon and Kendra Bischoff, "Growth in the Residential Segregation of Families by Income, 1970–2009," Russell Sage Foundation, November 2011. http://www.scribd.com/doc/72915429/Growth-in-the-Residential-Segregation-of-Families-by-Income-1970-2009.

22. Jennifer L. Hochschild, *Facing Up to the American Dream*, 48.

23. Hochschild, *Facing Up to the American Dream*, 45.

24. Pallavi Mathur, "Claiming Admissions Data Trade Secrets—Taking Advantage or Statutory Ambiguity?" *Northwestern Journal of Technology and Intellectual Property* 115 (2019).

25. Jeffrey Selingo, *Who Gets In and Why: A Year Inside College Admissions* (Scribner, 2020).

26. Richard H. Sander and Stuart Taylor Jr., *Mismatch: How Affirmative Action Hurts Students It's Intended to Help and Why Universities Won't Admit It* (Basic Books, 2012), 235.

27. Sander and Taylor Jr., *Mismatch*, 171.

28. Timothy Maguire, "My Bout with Affirmative Action," *Commentary* magazine, April 1992.

29. Maguire, "My Bout with Affirmative Action."

30. Thomas J. Kane, "Racial and Ethnic Preferences in College Admissions," in Christopher Jencks and Meredith Phillips, eds., *The Black-White Test Score Gap*, (Brookings Institution Press, 1998), 432.

31. Richard J. Herrnstein and Charles Murray, *The Bell Curve: Intelligence and Class Structure in American Life* (Free Press Paperbacks, 1996), 447.

32. Ibram X. Kendi, *How to Be an Antiracist* (One World, 2023), 113.

33. Kendi, *How to Be an Antiracist*, 112.

34. Abigail Thernstrom and Stephan Thernstrom, *No Excuses: Closing the Racial Gap in Learning* (Simon & Schuster, 2003), 88–90; Jason L. Riley, *Please Stop*

Helping Us: How Liberals Make It Harder for Blacks to Succeed (Encounter Books, 2014), 49–50.

35. John U. Ogbu, *Black American Students in an Affluent Suburb: A Study of Academic Disengagement* (Lawrence Erlbaum Associates, 2003), 35.

36. John U. Ogbu, *Black American Students in an Affluent Suburb*, 23.

37. "Parenting in America: Choose Your Parents Wisely," *The Economist*, July 26, 2014.

38. Leila Morsy and Richard Rothstein, "Five Social Disadvantages That Depress Student Performance," Education Policy Institute, June 10, 2015. https://www.epi.org/publication/five-social-disadvantages-that-depress-student-performance-why-schools-alone-cant-close-achievement-gaps/.

39. Reema Amin and Becky Vevea, "More Chicago Students Met Reading and Math Standards in 2022–23, Data Show," *Chalkbeat Chicago*, September 19, 2023.

40. Claude M. Steele, "Race and the Schooling of Black Americans," *The Atlantic*, April 1992.

41. Robert Klitgaard, *Choosing Elites* (Basic Books, 1985), 108.

42. Klitgaard, *Choosing Elites*, 108.

43. Klitgaard, *Choosing Elites*, 161.

44. Donald Wittman, "The University of California Was Wrong to Abolish the SAT: Admissions When Affirmative Action Was Banned," *Educational Measurement: Issues and Practice*, Summer 2024, 42, no. 2, 55–63.

45. John H. Bunzel, "Affirmative-Action Admissions: How It 'Works' at UC Berkeley," *National Affairs, The Public Interest*, Fall 1988.

46. William G. Bowen and Derek Bok, *The Shape of the River: Long-Term Consequences of Considering Race in College and University Admissions* (Princeton University Press, 1998), 18–19.

47. Arthur Hu, "Minorities Need More Support," *The Tech*, March 17, 1987.

48. Claude M. Steele, "Race and the Schooling of Black Americans," *The Atlantic*, April 1992.

49. Richard J. Herrnstein and Charles Murray, *The Bell Curve* (Free Press, 1994), 779.

50. Sander and Taylor Jr., *Mismatch*, 163–166, 235

51. "The Facts About Affirmative Action," *New York Times*, September 14, 1998.

52. "Race Panel's Lost Chance," *Los Angeles Times*, September 21, 1998.

53. Bowen and Bok, *The Shape of the River*, 276.

54. Sander and Taylor Jr., *Mismatch*, 236.

55. Sander and Taylor Jr., *Mismatch*, 239.

56. Stephan Thernstrom and Abigail Thernstrom, "Reflections on *The Shape of the River*," *UCLA Law Review*, June 1999, 1589.

57. Thernstrom and Thernstrom, "Reflections on *The Shape of the River*," 1594, 1595.

58. Thernstrom and Thernstrom, "Reflections on *The Shape of the River*," 1605.

59. Thomas Sowell, *Affirmative Action Around the World: An Empirical Study* (Yale University Press, 2004), 152–153.

60. Thernstrom and Thernstrom, "Reflections on *The Shape of the River*," 1606.

61. Thernstrom and Thernstrom, "Reflections on *The Shape of the River*," 1607, 1608.

62. Thernstrom and Thernstrom, "Reflections on *The Shape of the River*," 1608.

63. Peter Arcidiacono, Esteban M. Aucejo, and Ken Spenner, "What Happens After Enrollment? An Analysis of The Time Path of Racial Differences in GPA and Major Choice," *IZA Journal of Labor Economics*, 2012, 1:5.

64. Frederick L. Smith and John J. McArdle, "Ethnic and Gender Differences in Science Graduation at Selective Colleges with Implications for Admissions Policy and College Choice," *Research in Higher Education*, 45, no. 4, June 2004.

65. Arcidiacono, Aucejo, and Spenner, "What Happens After Enrollment?"

66. Sander and Taylor Jr., *Mismatch*, 231.

67. Stephen Cole and Elinor Barber, *Increasing Faculty Diversity: The Occupational Choices of High-Achieving Minority Students* (Harvard University Press, 2003), 124. (Citations omitted.)

68. Cole and Barber, *Increasing Faculty Diversity*, 30.

69. Gail Heriot and Maimon Schwarzschild, eds. *A Dubious Expediency: How Race Preferences Damage Higher Education*, (Encounter Books, 2021), 66–67.

70. Clyde W. Summers, "Preferential Admissions: An Unreal Solution to a Real Problem," *Toledo Law Review*, Spring/Summer 1970, 379.

71. Summers, "Preferential Admissions," 379.

72. Summers, "Preferential Admissions," 384.

73. Summers, "Preferential Admissions," 395.

74. Bowen and Bok, *The Shape of the River*, 116.

75. Cole and Barber, *Increasing Faculty Diversity*, 206.

76. National Research Council, 1998, *Summary Report 1996: Doctorate Recipients from United States Universities*, Washington, DC: The National Academies Press. https://doi.org/10.17226/9530.

77. Tamar Jacoby, "Color Blind," *New Republic*, March 29, 1999.

78. Uché Blackstock, "How Thousands of Black U.S. Doctors Simply Vanished," *Washington Post*, January 28, 2024.

79. "PISA 2022 Results (Volume I): The State of Learning and Equity in Education," Organization for Economic Co-operation and Development, December 5, 2023. https://www.oecd.org/en/publications/pisa-2022-results-volume-i_53f23 881-en/full-report/component-6.html#introduction-d5e841.

80. Cole and Barber, *Increasing Faculty Diversity*, 249.

81. Richard Pérez-Peña, "In California, Early Push for College Diversity," *New York Times*, May 8, 2013.

82. Sander and Taylor Jr., *Mismatch*, 154.

83. Sander and Taylor Jr., *Mismatch*, 152–153.

84. Alison Mitchell, "Defending Affirmative Action, Clinton Urges Debate on Race," *New York Times*, June 15, 1997.

Chapter 6: Conclusion

1. Charles Campisi, "The Myth of the Trigger-Happy Cop," *Wall Street Journal*, February 2, 2017.

2. Dan McLaughlin, "Watch Judicial Nominee Nusrat Choudhury," *National Review*, April 29, 2022. https://www.nationalreview.com/corner/watch-judicial-nominee-nusrat-choudhury-self-destruct-under-questioning-by-senator-john-kennedy/.

3. "Fatal Force," *Washington Post,* database accessed on October 24, 2024. https://www.washingtonpost.com/graphics/investigations/police-shootings-database/.

4. Emma Colton, "Massive Increase in Black Americans Murdered Was Result of Defund the Police Movement: Experts," *Fox News*, April 19, 2022; "Number of Murder Victims in the United States in 2022, by Race," *Statista Research Department,* July 5, 2024.

5. Heather Mac Donald, *When Race Trumps Merit: How the Pursuit of Equity Sacrifices Excellence, Destroys Beauty, and Threatens Lives* (DW Books, 2023), 211.

6. Wilfred Reilly, *Taboo: 10 Facts You Can't Talk About* (Regnery Publishing, 2020), xv–xvi.

7. Tanaya Devi and Roland G. Fryer, "Policing the Police: The Impact of 'Pattern-or-Practice' Investigations on Crime," National Bureau of Economic Research, Working Paper No. 27324, June 2020. https://www.nber.org/system/files/working_papers/w27324/w27324.pdf.

8. Zusha Elinson, "U.S. Murders Up Nearly 30% in 2020, FBI Says," *Wall Street Journal*, September 28, 2021.

9. Del Quentin Wilbur, "Homicide Rate Rises for a Second Year," *Wall Street Journal*, September 26, 2017.

10. "DOJ Clears Darren Wilson in Michael Brown Killing," *CBS News*, March 4, 2015.

11. Troy Closson, "With Rise in Shootings, a Wave of Grief for New York's Children," *New York Times*, April 28, 2022.

12. Kim Barker, Steve Eder, Julie Tate, "License Plate Mismatch Ends in Fatal Shooting," *New York Times*, April 28, 2022.

13. "Fatal Force," *Washington Post,* database accessed on October 24, 2024. https://www.washingtonpost.com/graphics/investigations/police-shootings-database/

14. Rob Hayes, "More law enforcement officers are being shot around the country, police groups says," *ABC7 Los Angeles*, January 4, 2024.

15. "Are You With Biden or Jefferson Davis?" *Wall Street Journal*, January 12, 2022.

16. "Blacks Voted at a Higher Rate than Whites—A First, Census Bureau Reports," U.S. Census Bureau, May 8, 2013; Rachel Weiner, "Black Voters Turned Out at a Higher Rate Than White Voters in 2012 and 2008," *Washington Post*, April 29, 2013.

17. Jens Manuel Krogstad, Luis Noe-Bustamante, and Antonio Flores, "Historic Highs in 2018 Voter Turnout Extended across Racial and Ethnic Groups," *Pew Research Center*, May 1, 2019.

18. "Number of Voters and Voter Registration as a Share of the Voter Population," Kaiser Family Foundation, November 2022. https://www.kff.org/other/state-indicator/number-of-voters-and-voter-registration-in-thousands-as-a-share-of-the-voter-population/?currentTimeframe=0&sortModel=%7B%22colId%22:%22Location%22,%22sort%22:%22asc%22%7D.

19. Kyle Raze, "Voting Rights and the Resilience of Black Turnout," *Economic Inquiry*, July 2022.

20. Wesley Yang, "Harvard Is Wrong That Asians Have Terrible Personalities," *New York Times*, June 25, 2018.

21. John Yoo, "Facially Neutral, Racially Biased," *New Criterion*, September 22, 2022.

22. Anemona Hartocollis, "Decline in Asian Students Prompts Threat of Inquiry," *New York Times*, September 19, 2024.

23. "2023 SAT Suite of Assessments Annual Report," College Board. https://reports.collegeboard.org/media/pdf/2023-total-group-sat-suite-of-assessments-annual-report%20ADA.pdf.

24. William Julius Wilson, *The Truly Disadvantaged: The Inner City, the Underclass, and Public Policy* (University of Chicago Press, 1987), 110.

25. Michael D. Tanner, "Poverty and Welfare," Cato Handbook for Policymakers (2022). https://www.cato.org/cato-handbook-policymakers/cato-handbook-policymakers-9th-edition-2022/poverty-welfare.

26. Fred Siegel, *The Revolt Against the Masses: How Liberalism Has Undermined the Middle Class* (Encounter Books, 2013), 139.

27. Jody Miller, "Culture, Inequality, and Gender Relations Among Urban Black Youth," in Orlando Patterson and Ethan Fosse, eds., *The Cultural Matrix: Understanding Black Youth* (Harvard University Press, 2015), 380–382.

28. Jody Miller, *The Cultural Matrix*, 381, 383.

29. Robert L. Woodson Sr., "The Crucial Voice of '1776,'" *Red, White and Black: Rescuing American History from Revisionists and Race Hustlers* (Emancipation Books, 2021), xxiii.

30. Woodson Sr., *Red, White and Black*, xxiv.

31. William Julius Wilson, *The Truly Disadvantaged*, 3.

32. Sharon Nunn, "Labor-Force Race Gap All But Closes," *Wall Street Journal*, March 12, 2018.

33. Rafael A. Mangual et al., "Stronger Families, Safer Streets," *Institute for Family Studies*, December 12, 2023.

34. Kay Hymowitz, "New Insights Into the Poverty and Affluence Gap Among Major Racial and Ethnic Groups," *Institute for Family Studies*, February 26, 2019.

35. Orlando Patterson and Ethan Fosse, eds., *The Cultural Matrix: Understanding Black Youth* (Harvard University Press, 2015), 3.

36. Patterson and Fosse, *The Cultural Matrix: Understanding Black Youth*, 2.

37. Melissa S. Kearney, *The Two-Parent Privilege: How Americans Stopped Getting Married and Started Falling Behind* (University of Chicago Press, 2023), x.

38. Stephen J. Dubner, host, *Freakonomics Radio Book Club*, podcast, episode 19, "The Facts Are In: Two Parents Are Better Than One, September 21, 2023,"

https://freakonomics.com/podcast/when-did-marriage-become-a-luxury-good
-frbc/.

39. Cornel West, *The Cornel West Reader* (Basic Civita Books, 1999), 482.

40. Martha Bayles, *Hole in Our Soul: The Loss of Beauty and Meaning in American Popular Music* (University of Chicago Press, 1994), 356.

41. Katherine Sayer and Neil Shah, "Diddy's Diverse Empire Crumbles, but Warning Signs Were There," *Wall Street Journal*, June 7, 2024.

42. Janna Brancolini, "Diddy Asks for Gag Order After Witness Says He Has Shocking Tapes," *The Daily Beast*, November 4, 2024. https://www.thedailybeast
.com/sean-diddy-combs-requests-gag-order-after-witness-says-he-has-shocking
-videos/.

43. John McWhorter, *Woke Racism: How a New Religion Has Betrayed Black America* (Portfolio/Penguin, 2021), 81.

44. Eugene Robinson, "Jackson Asked the Right Thing on Affirmative Action," *Washington Post*, November 1, 2022.

45. Nicholas Confessore, "The Michigan Experiment," *New York Times Magazine*, October 20, 2024.

INDEX

JASON L. RILEY is a senior fellow at the Manhattan Institute and a columnist for the *Wall Street Journal*. He is the author of several previous books, including *Maverick: A Biography of Thomas Sowell*.